This book belongs to

Copyright by Mom&Me Publishing

All rights reserved. This book or any portion thereof may not

be reproduced or used in any manner whatsoever without

the express written permission of the publisher except

for the use of brief quotations in a book review. Recording of

this publicationis strictly prohibited and any storage

of this document is not allowed unless with written

from the publisher. All right reserved.

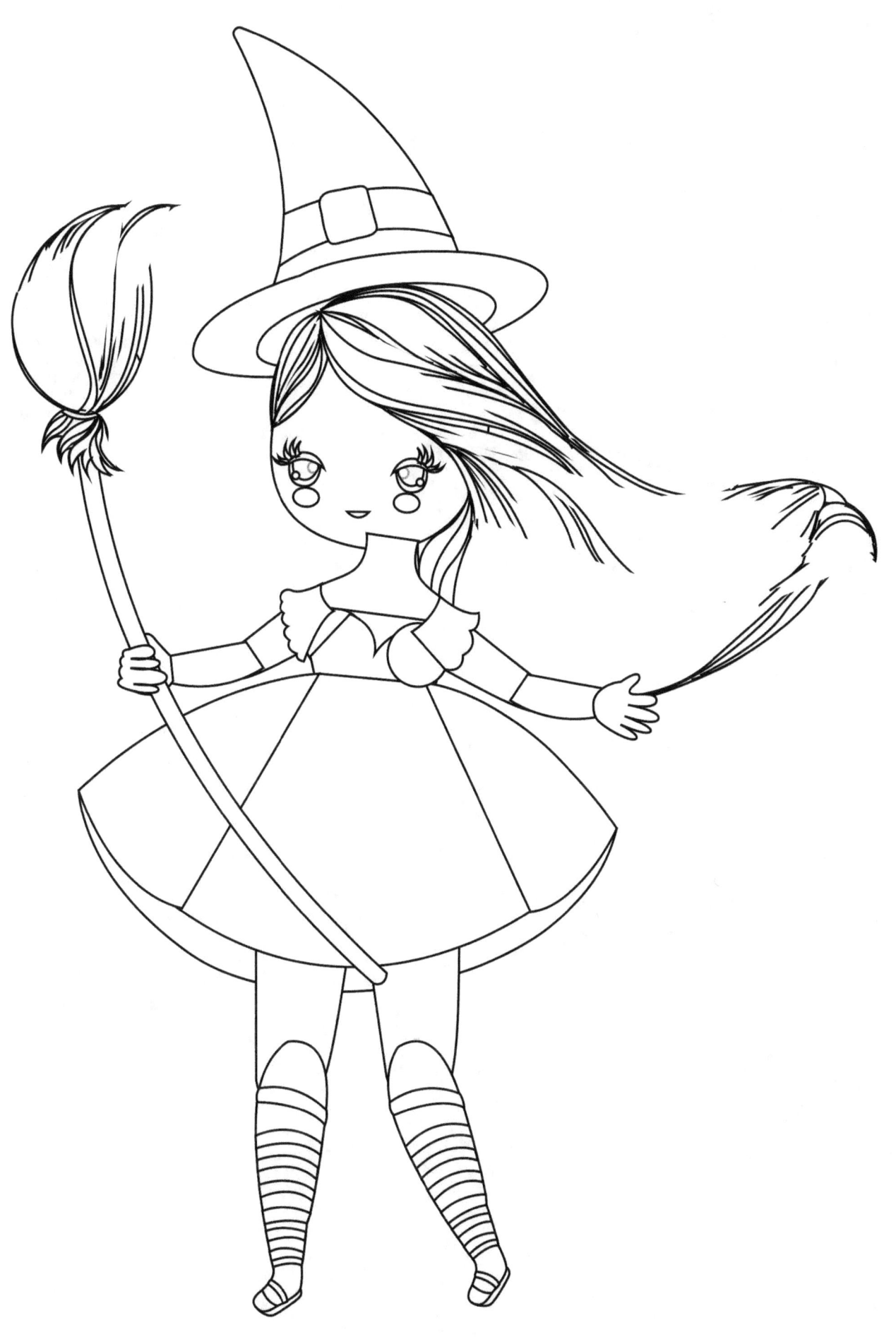

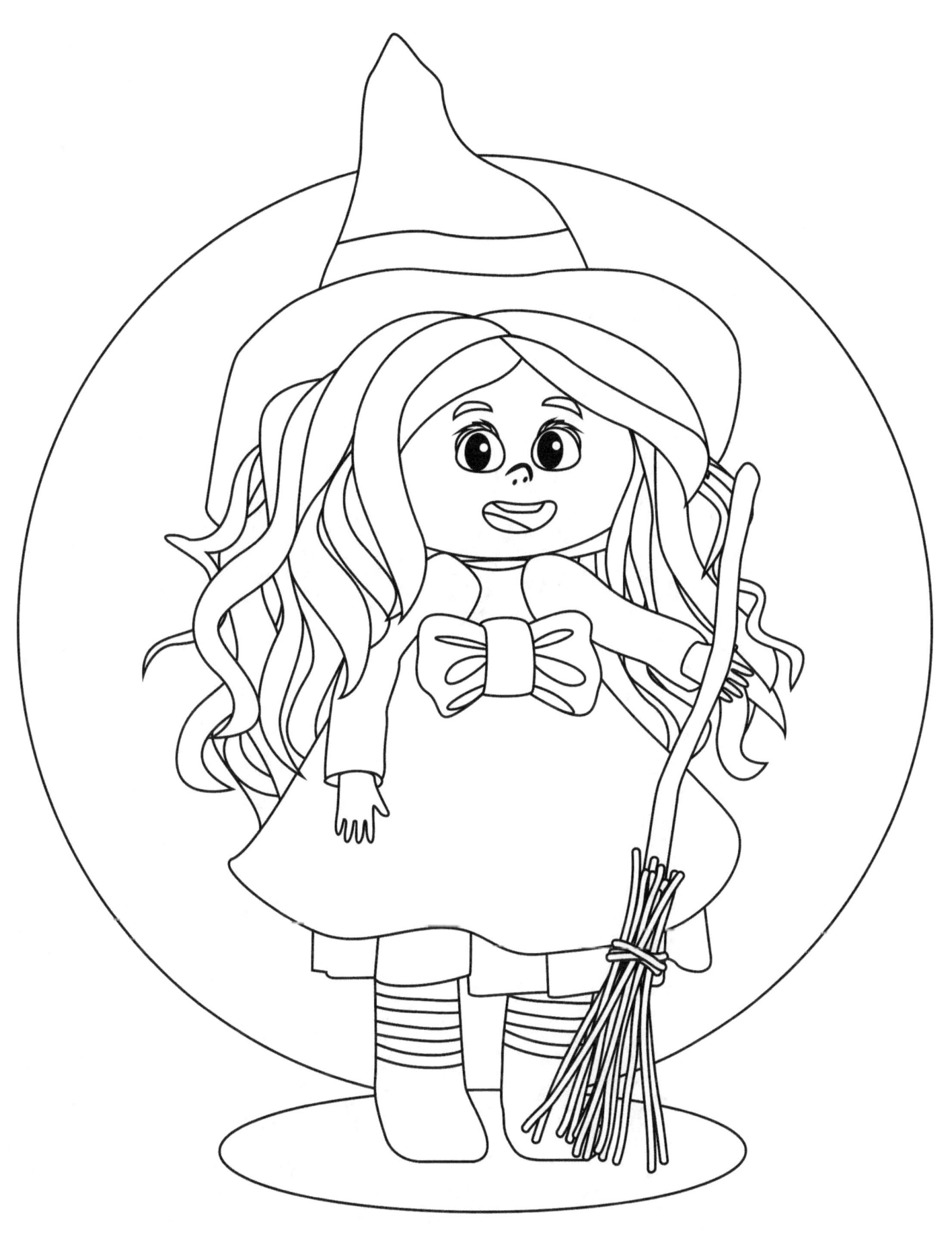

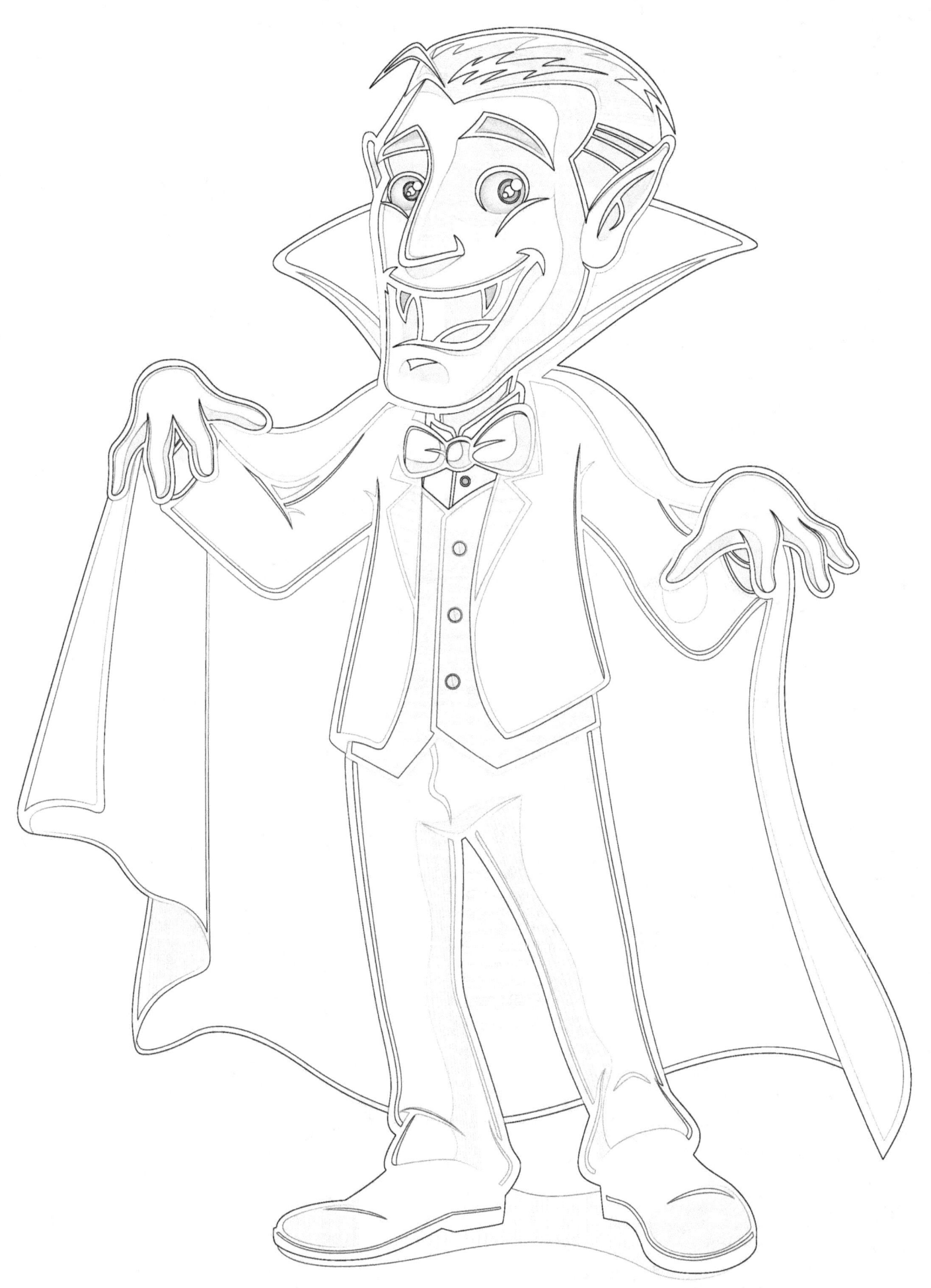

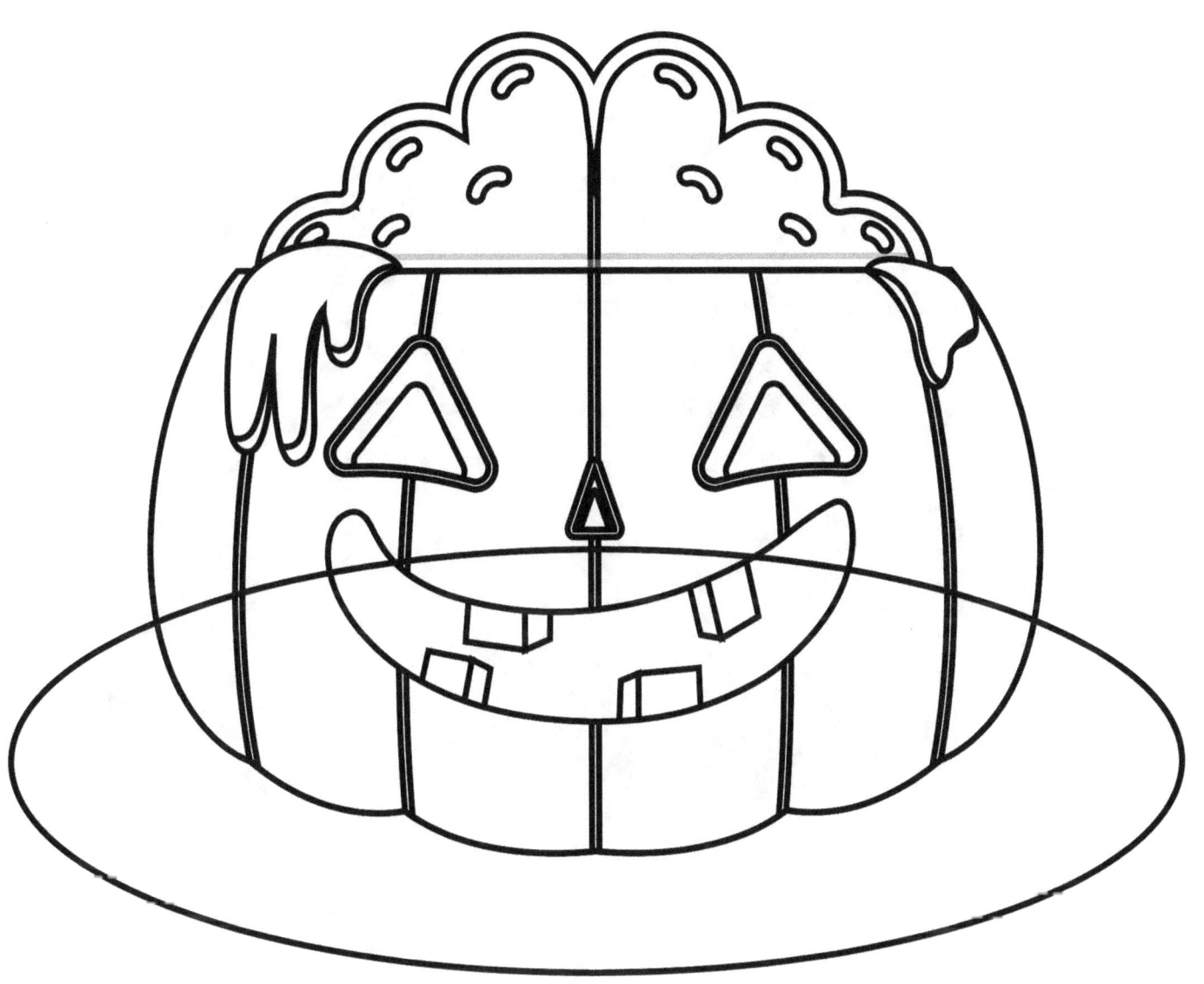

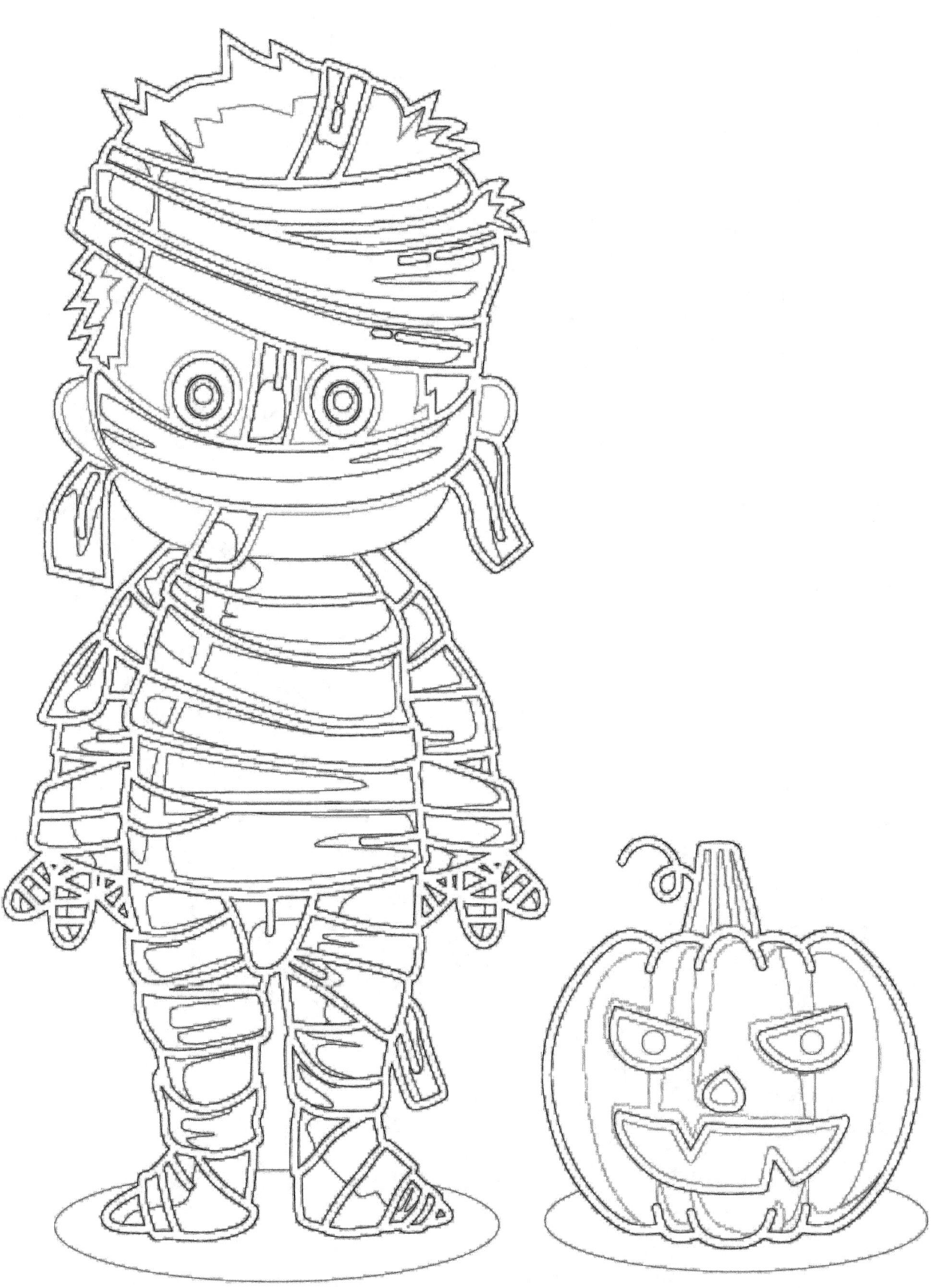

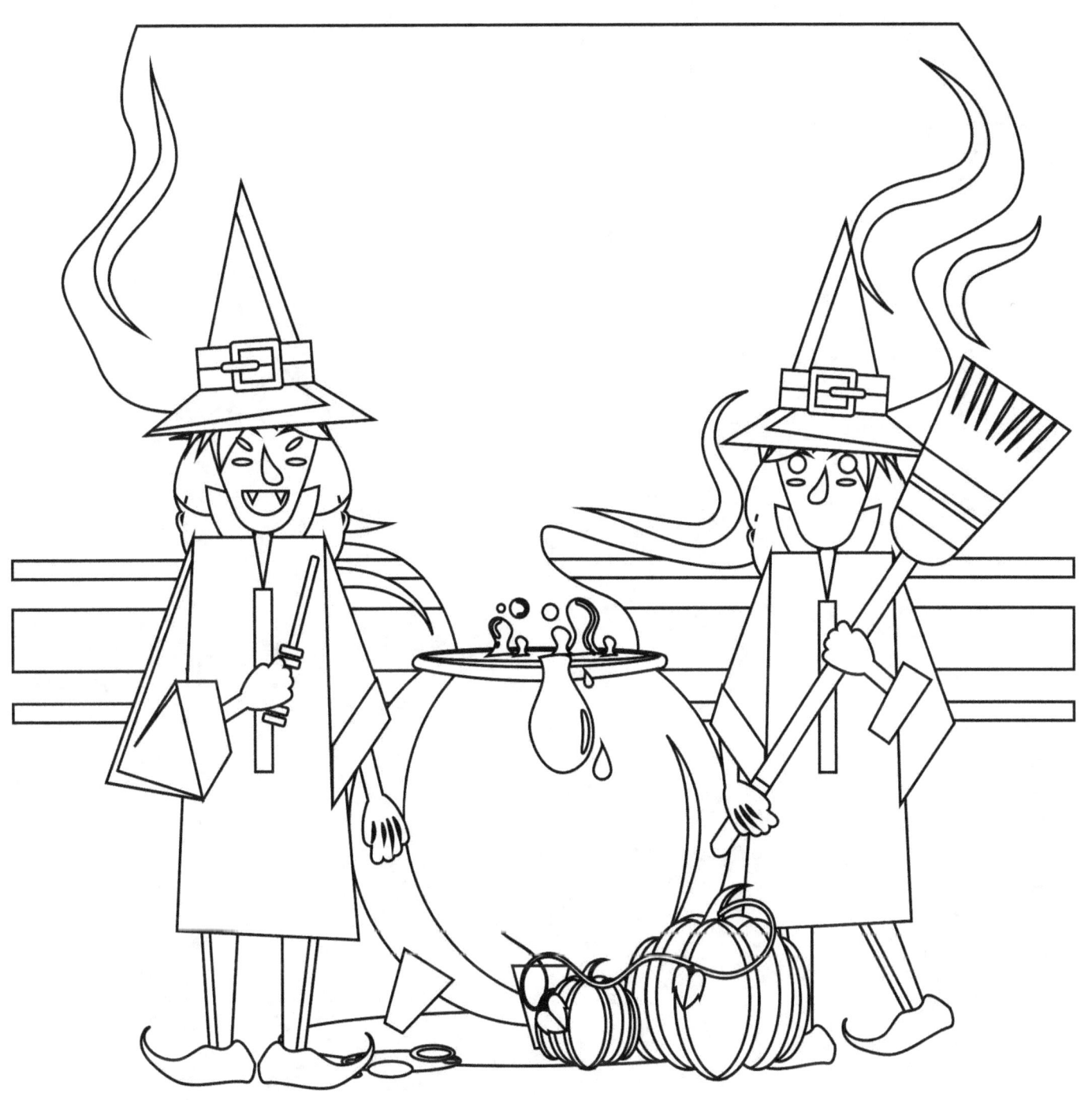

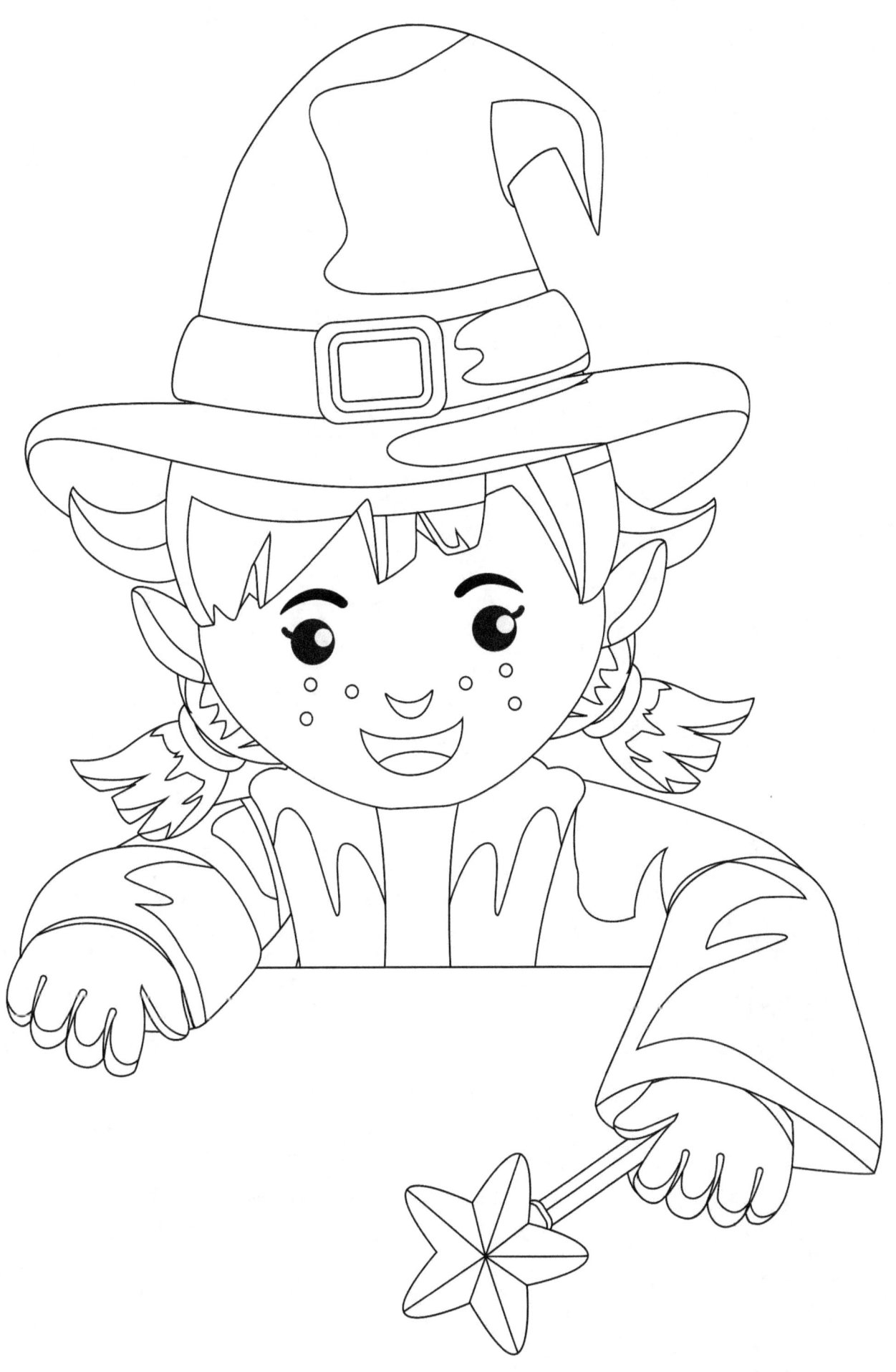

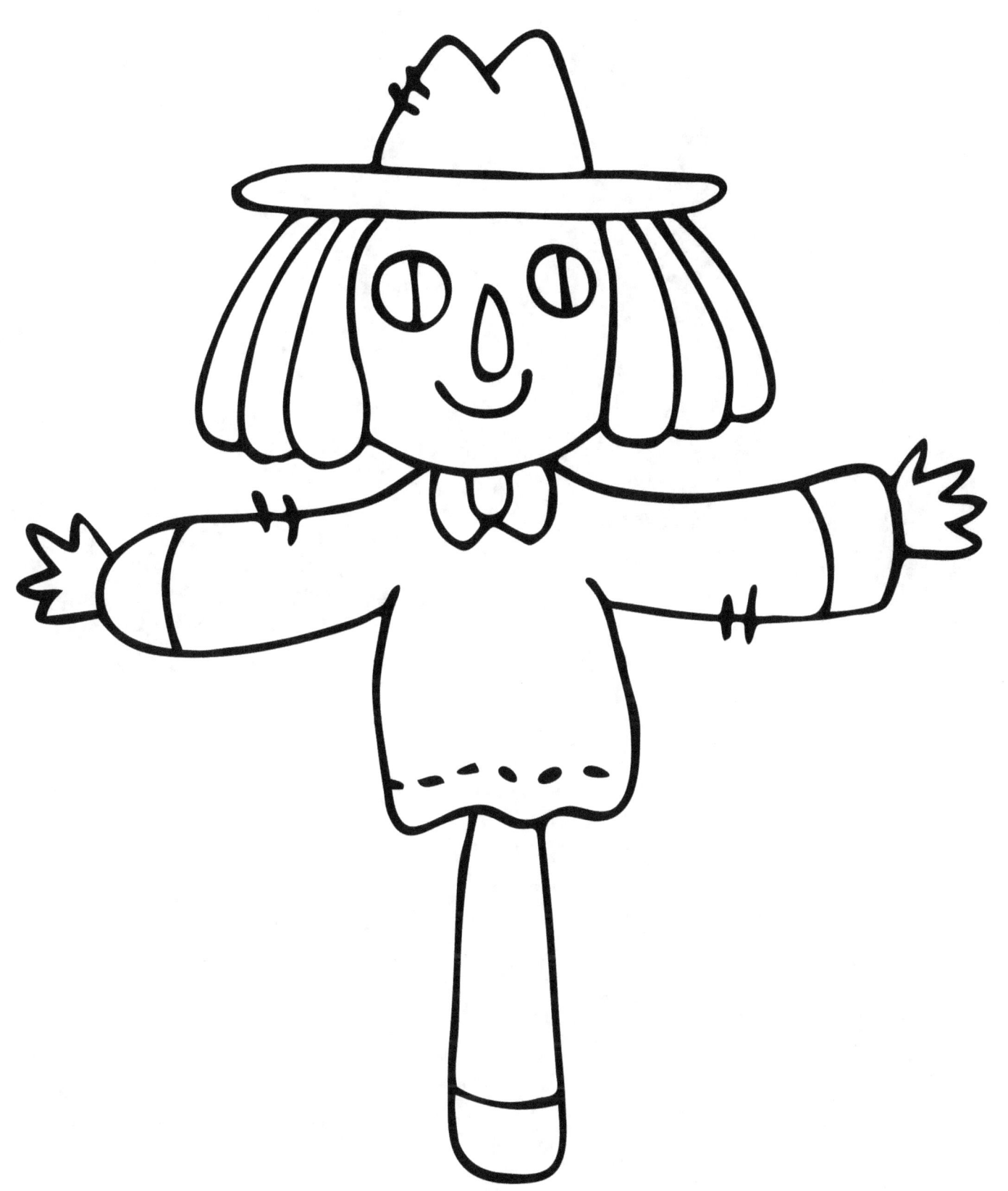

Happy Halloween

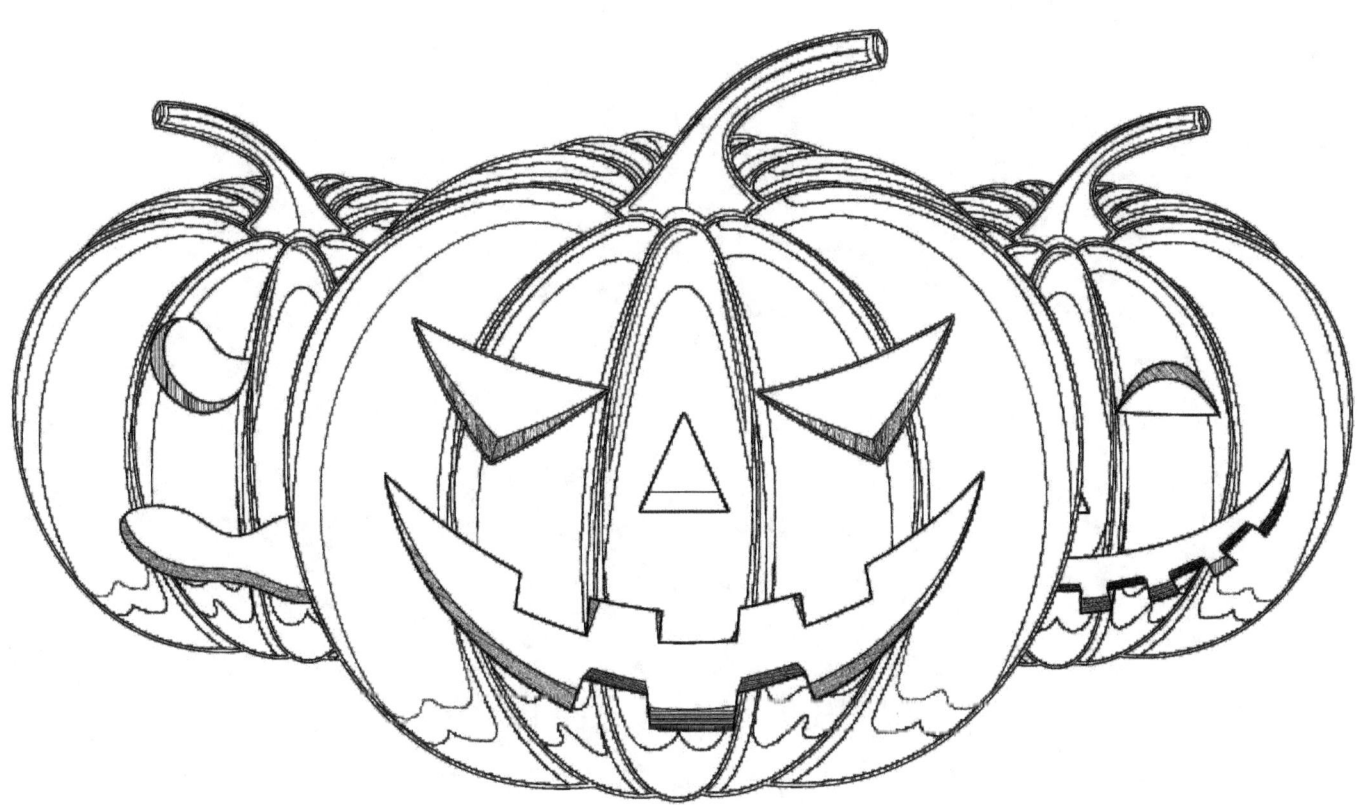

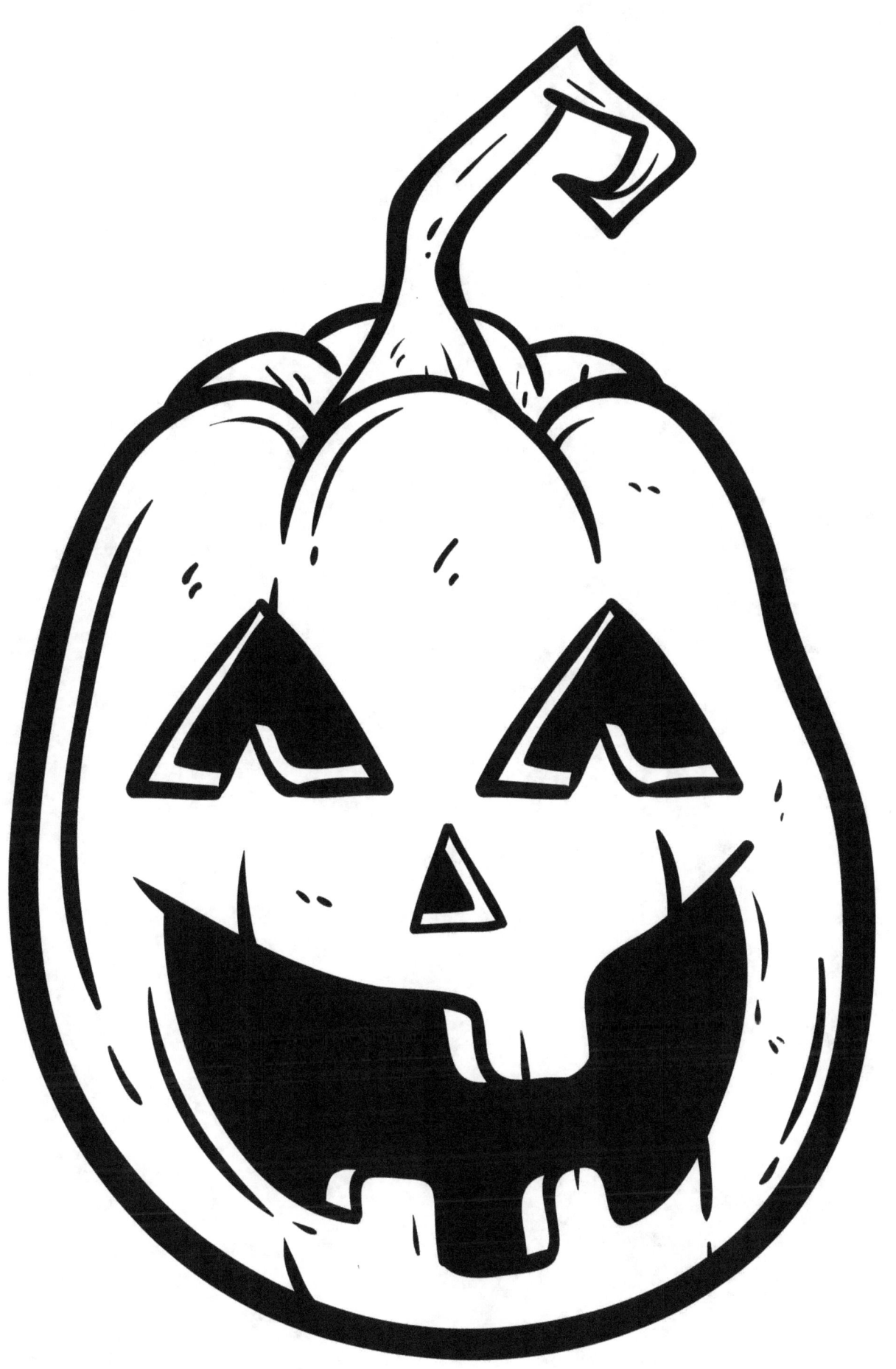

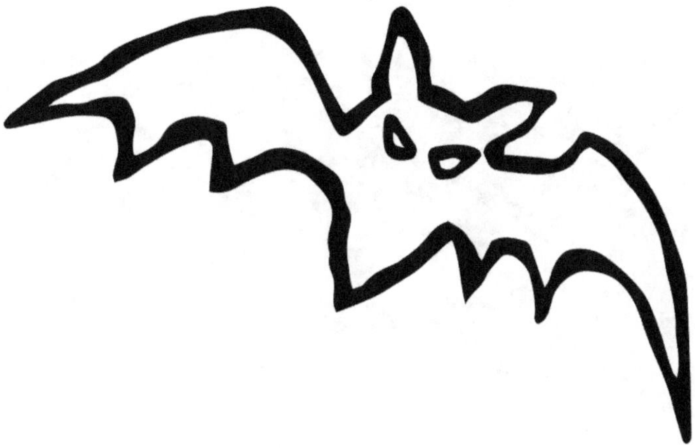

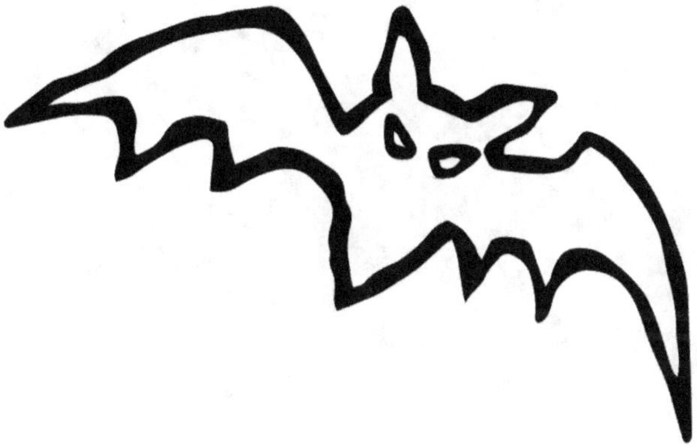

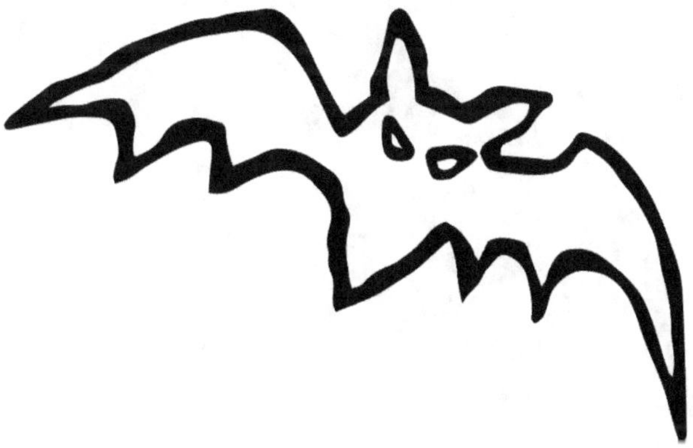

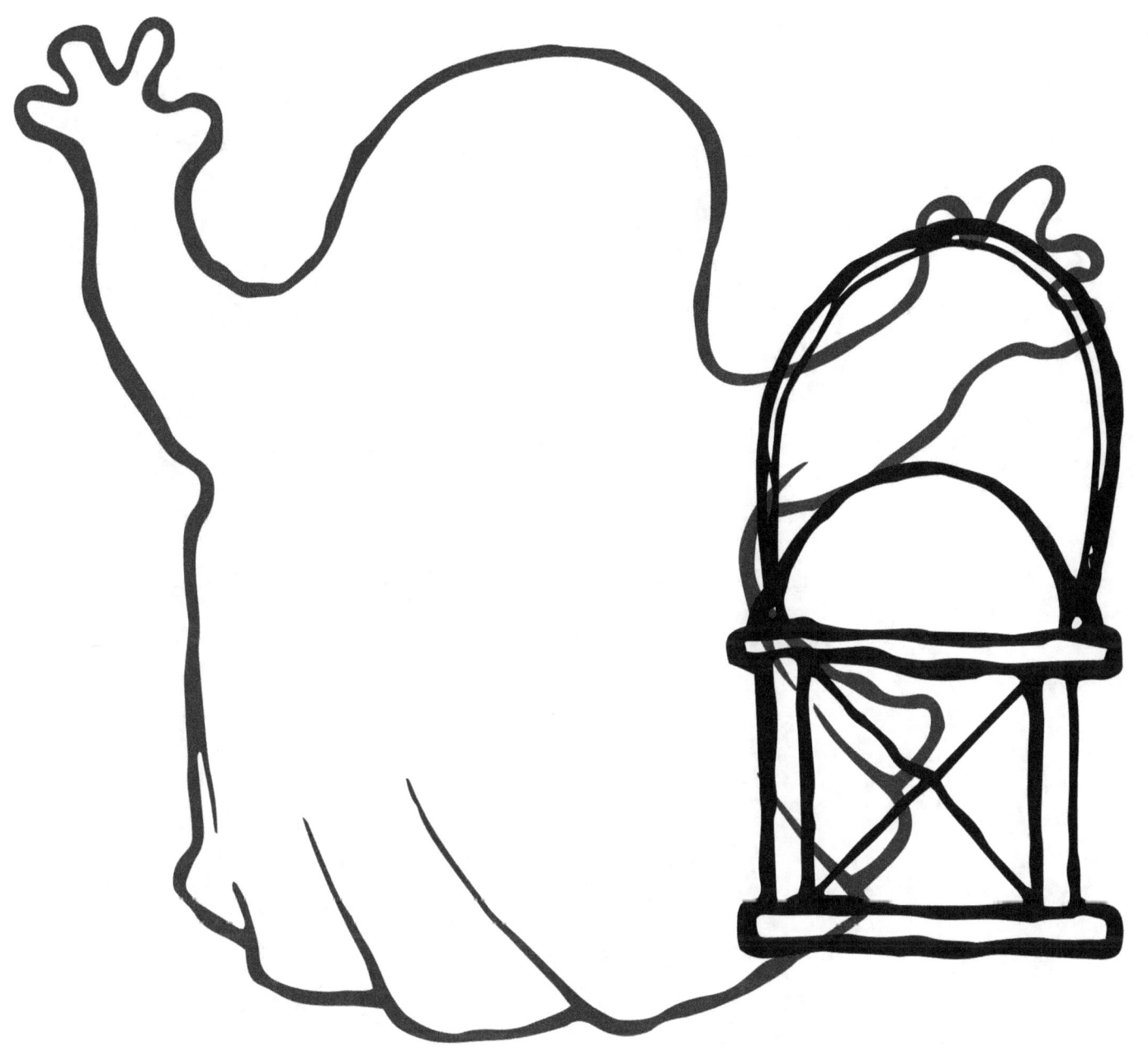

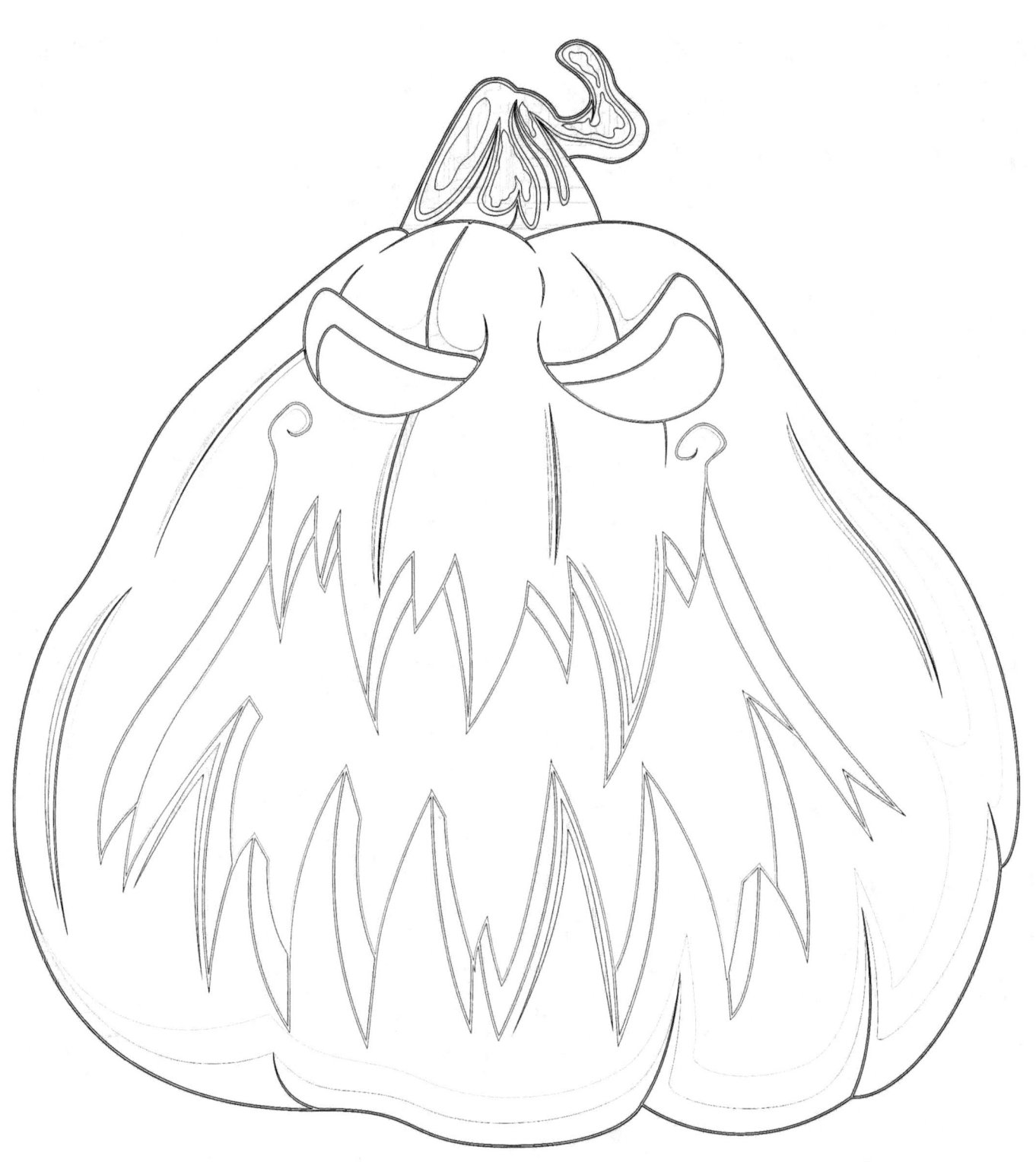

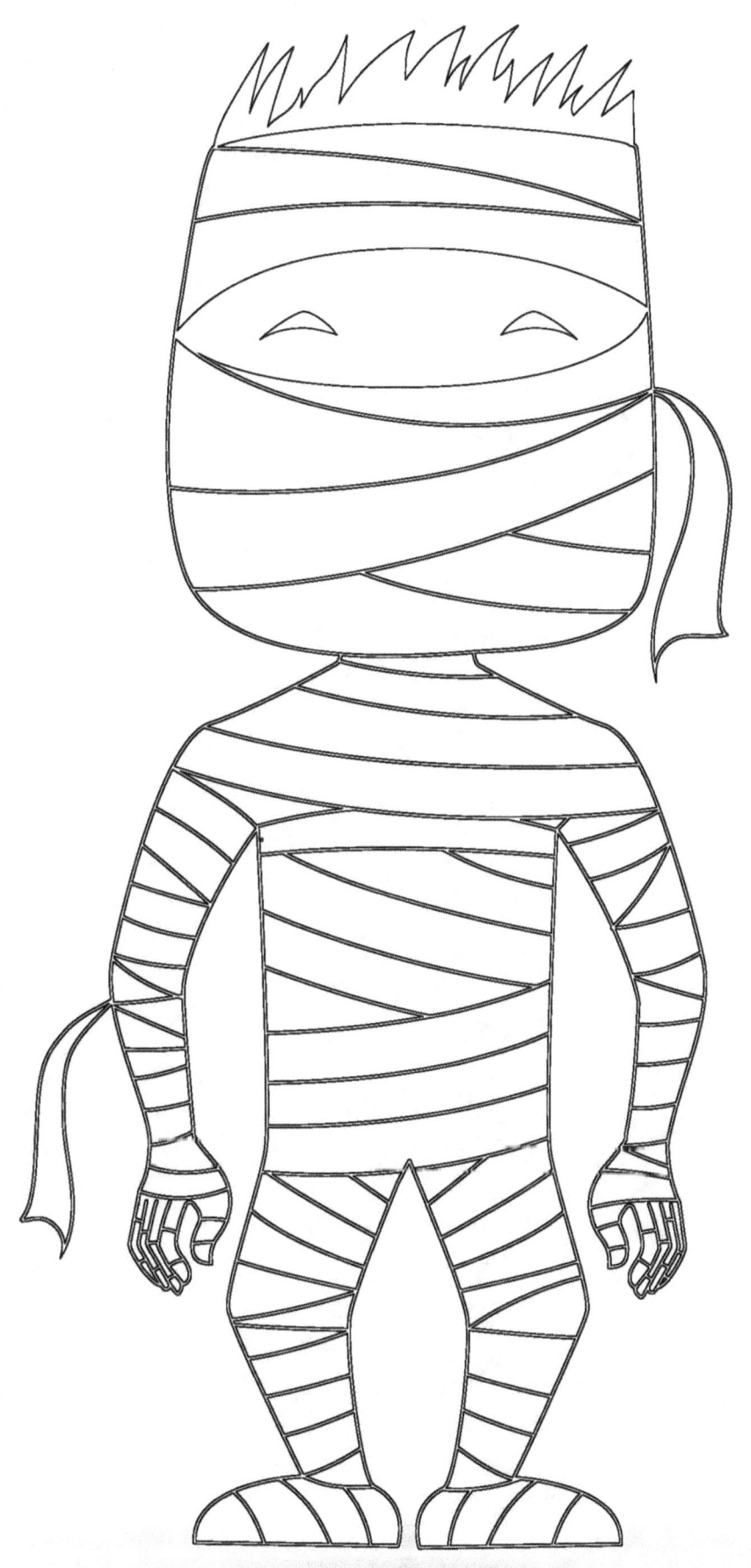

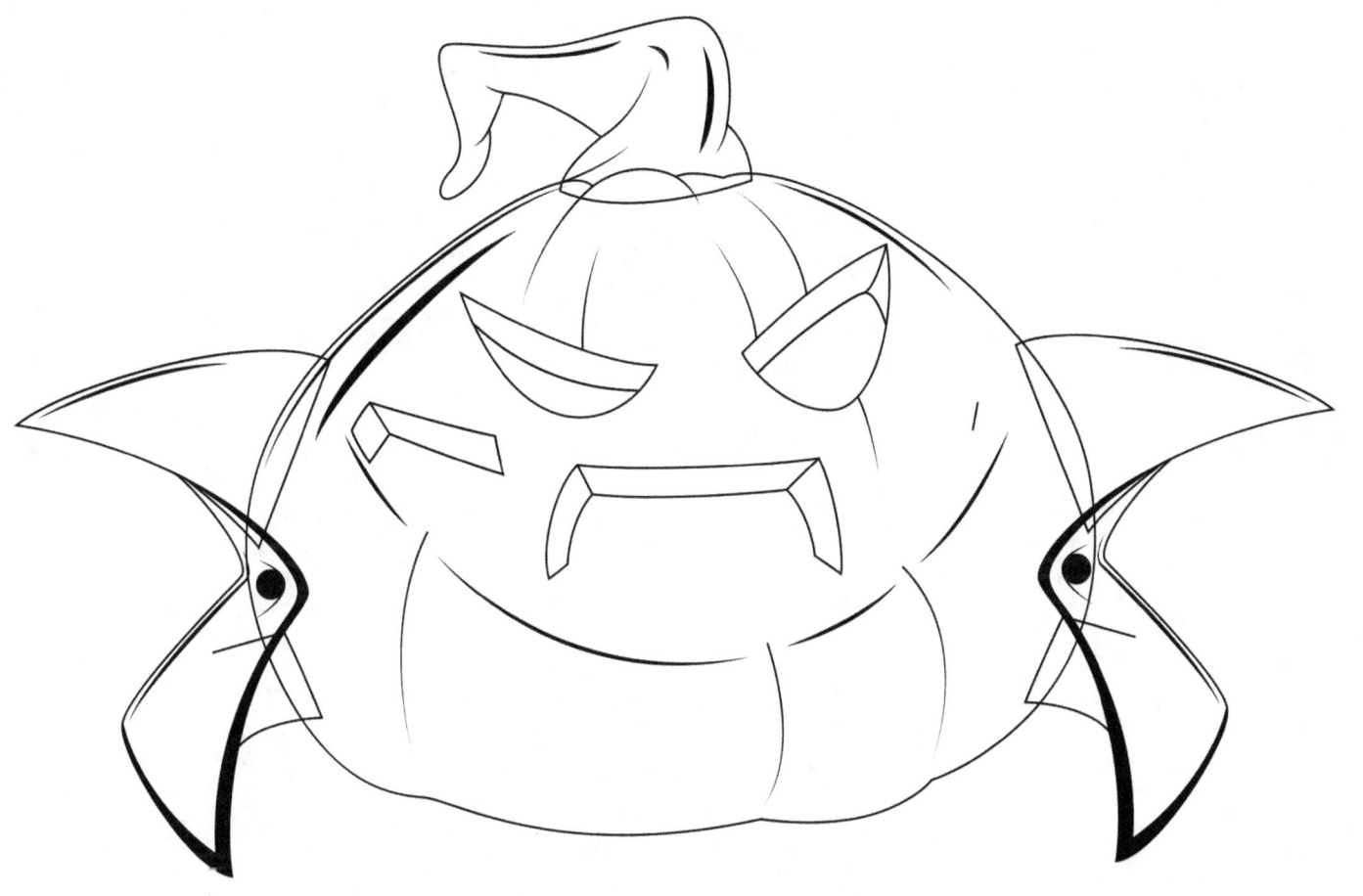

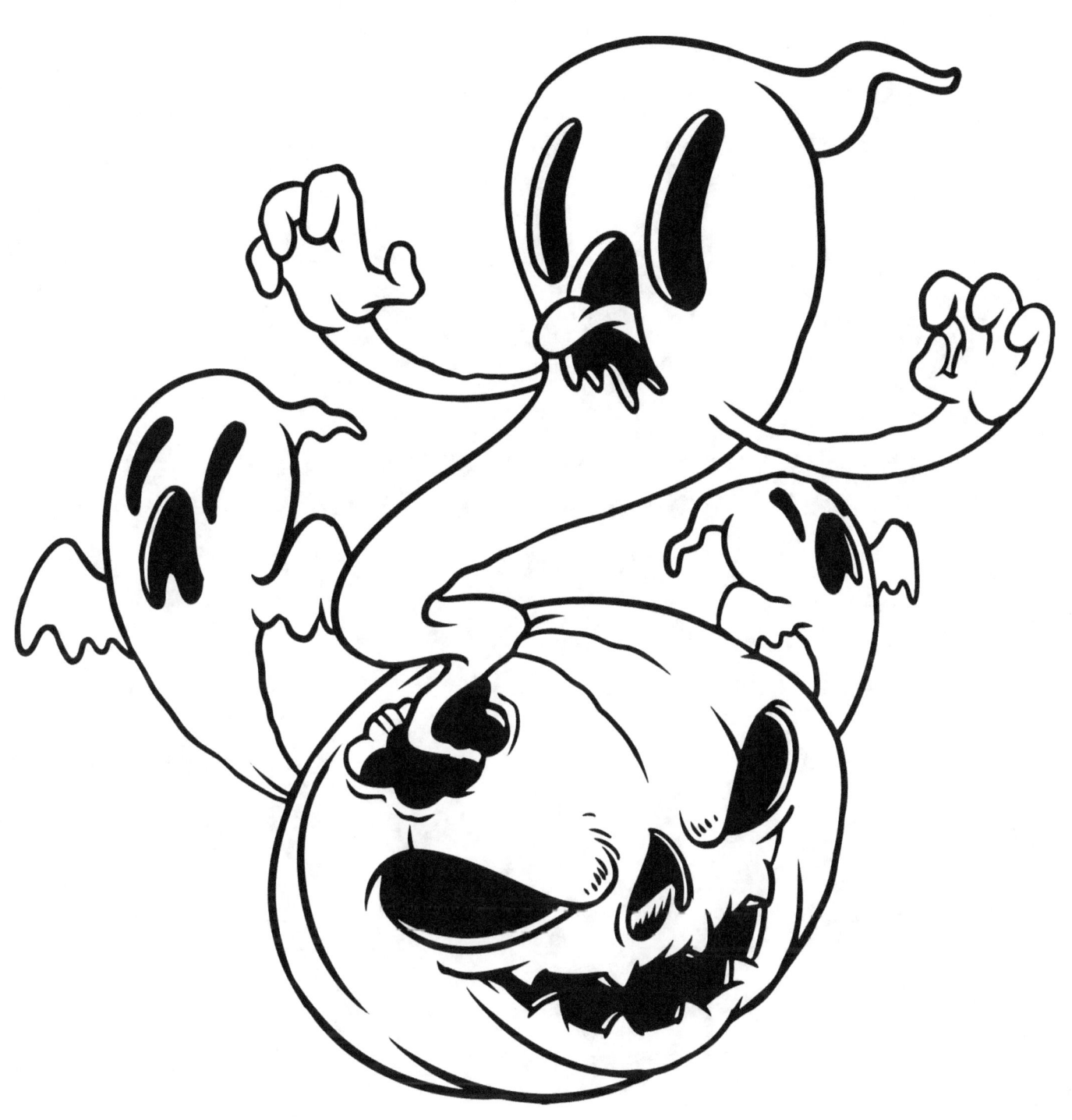

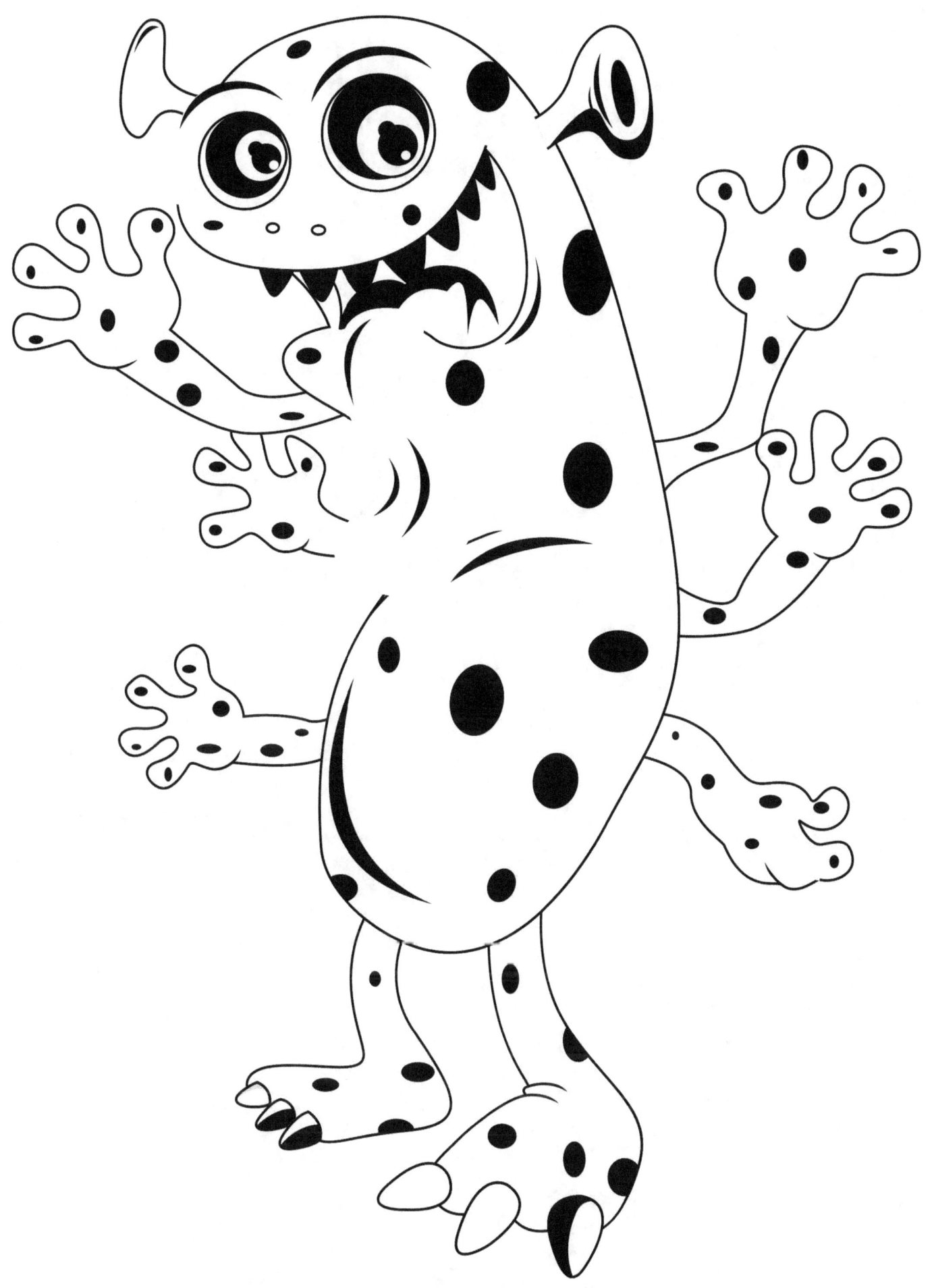

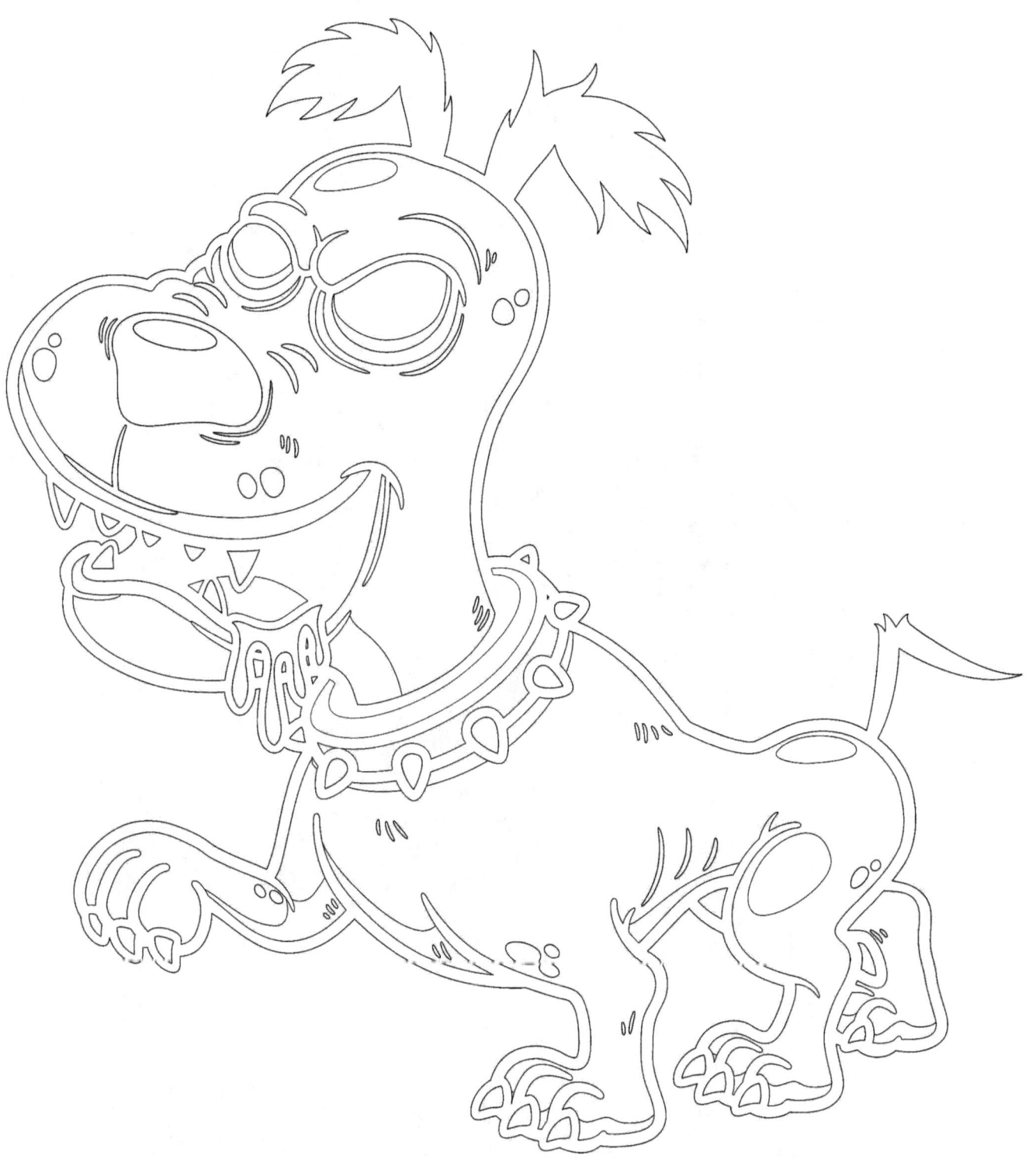

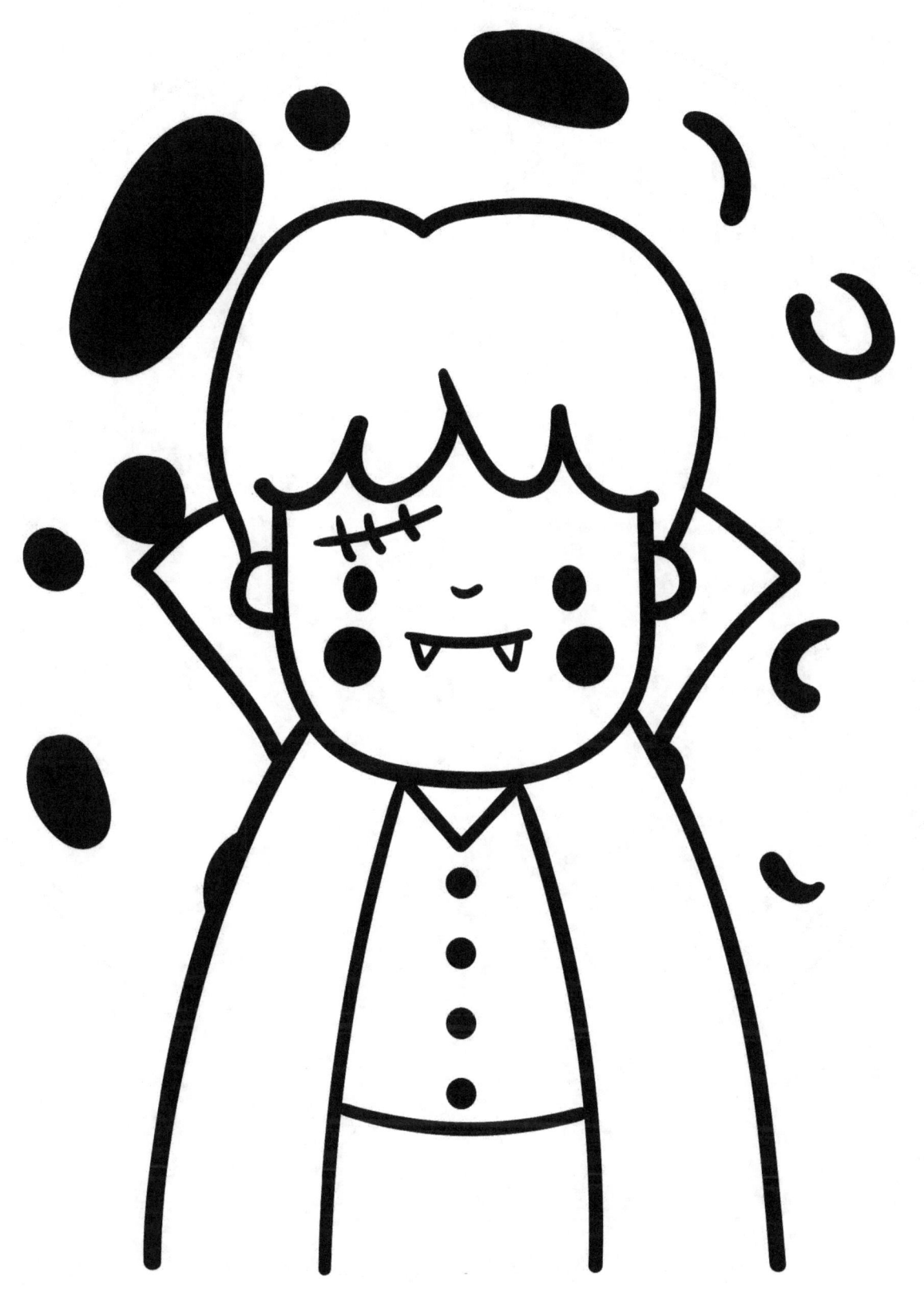

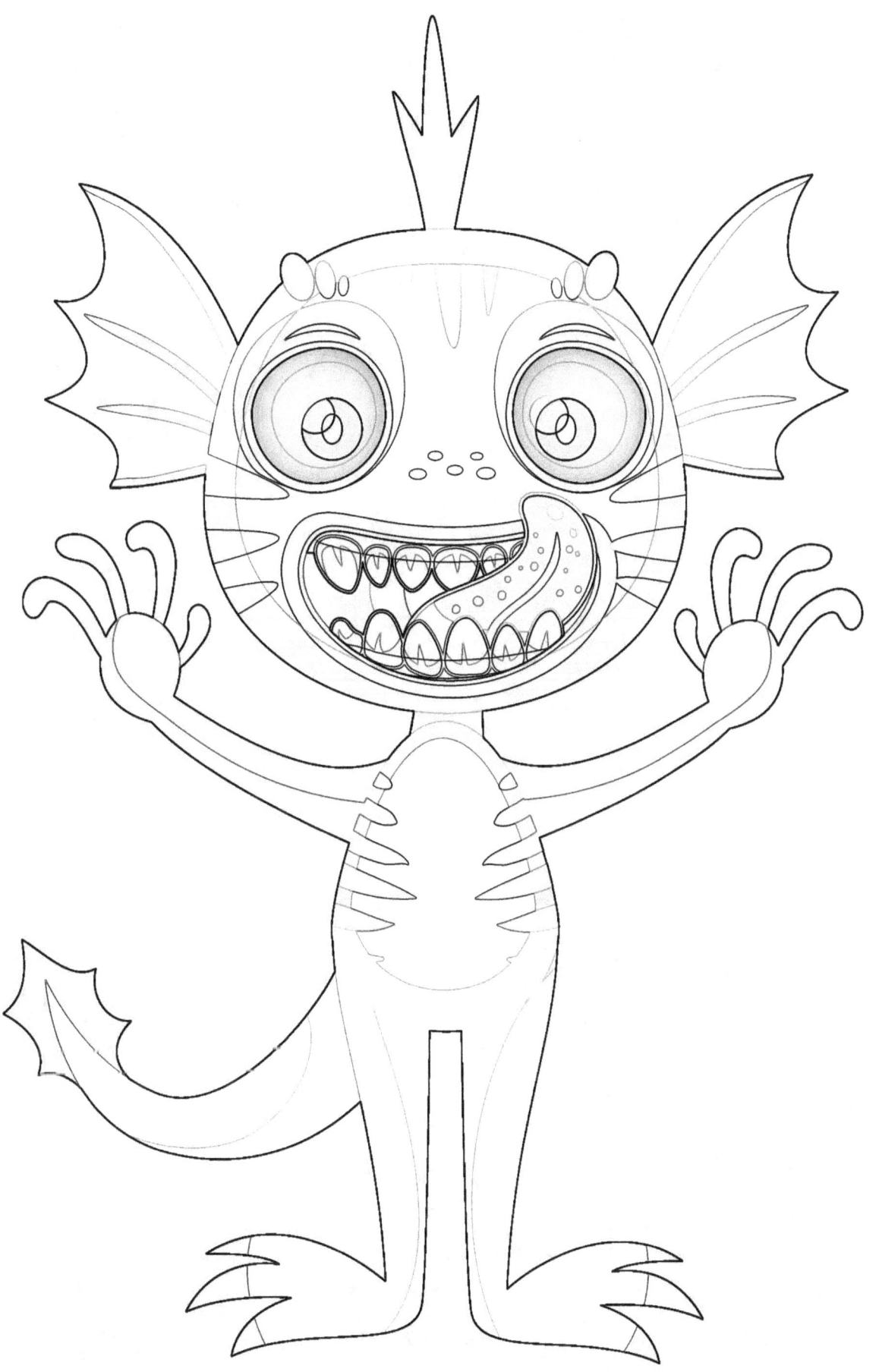

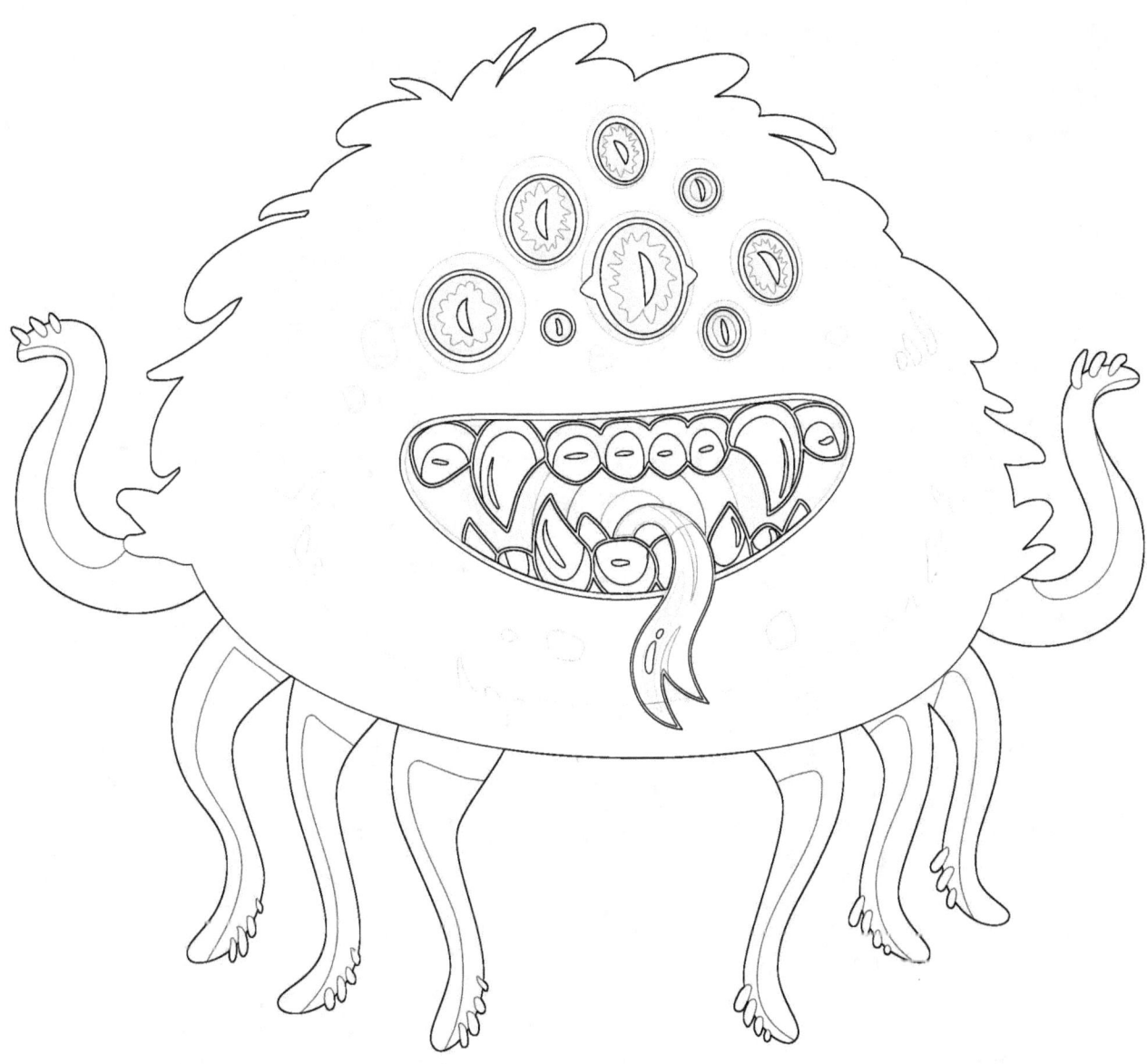

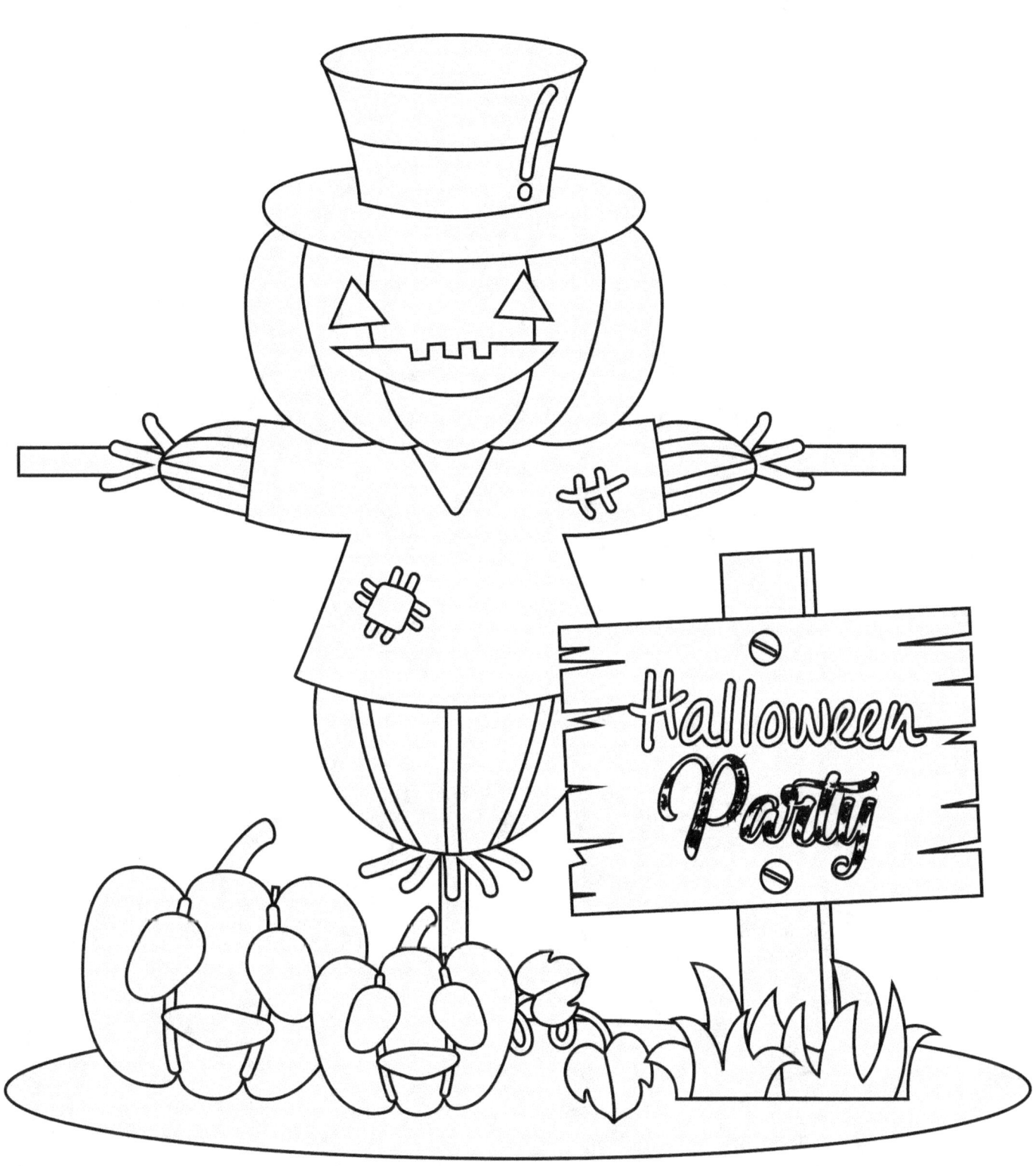

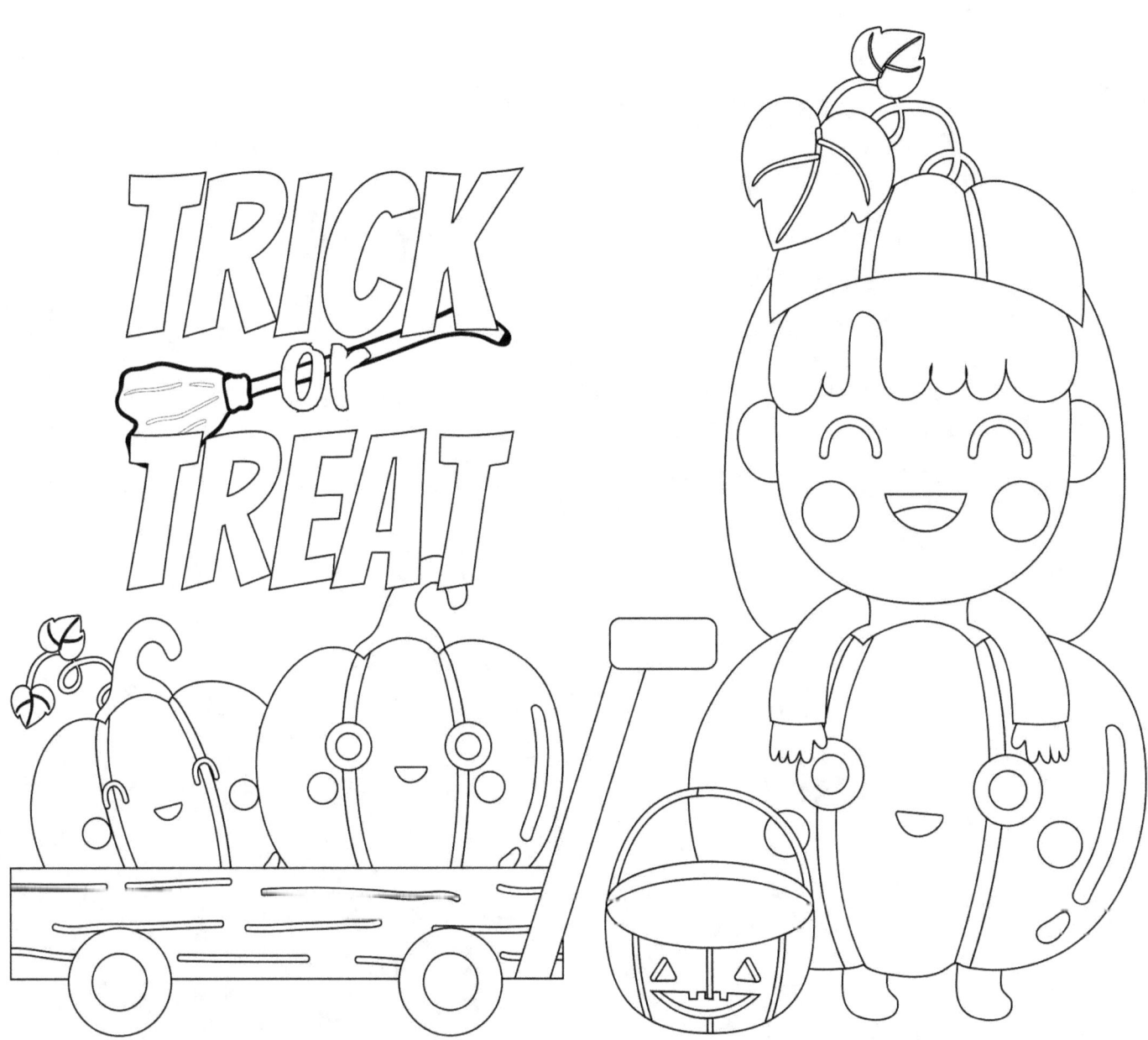

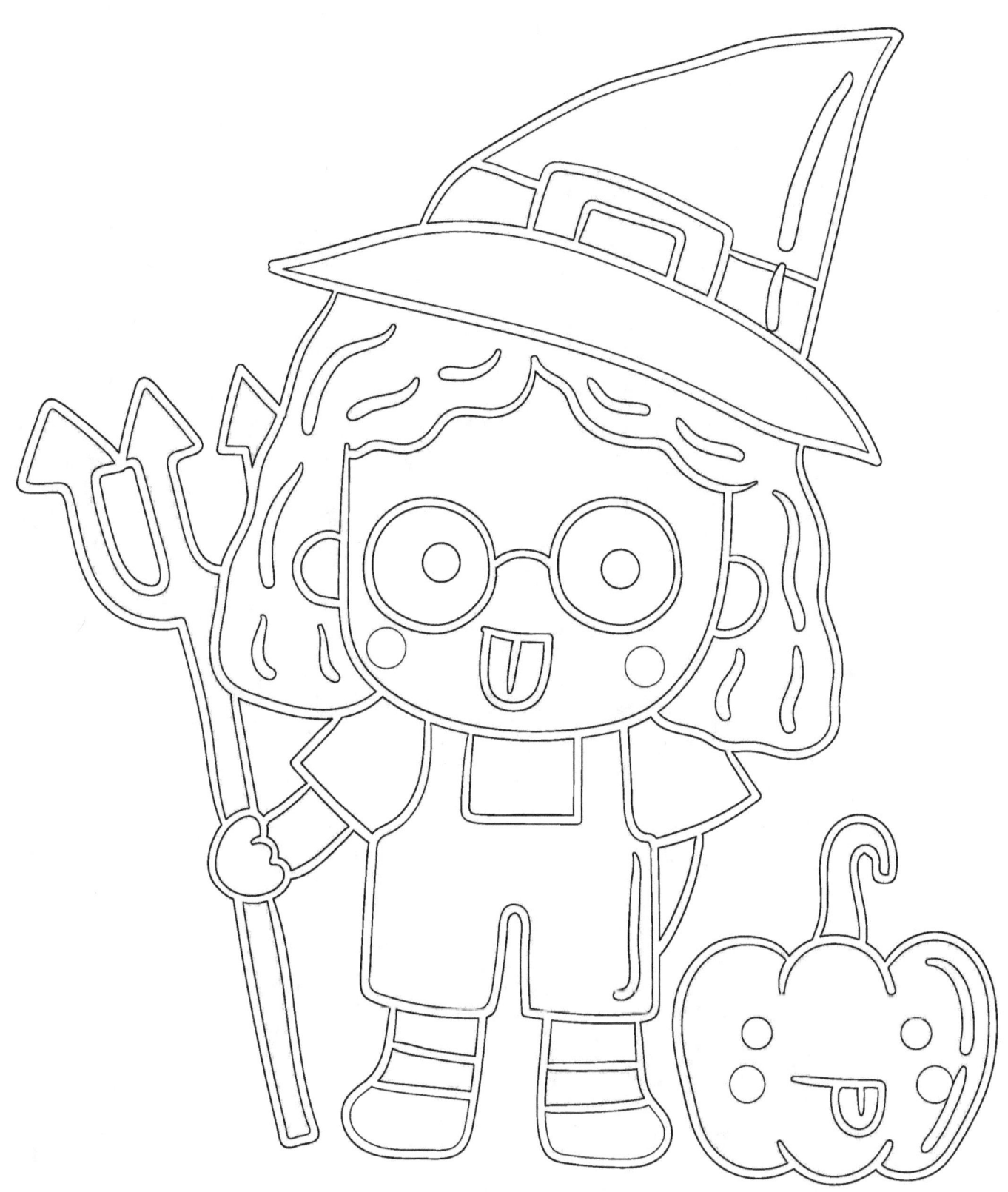

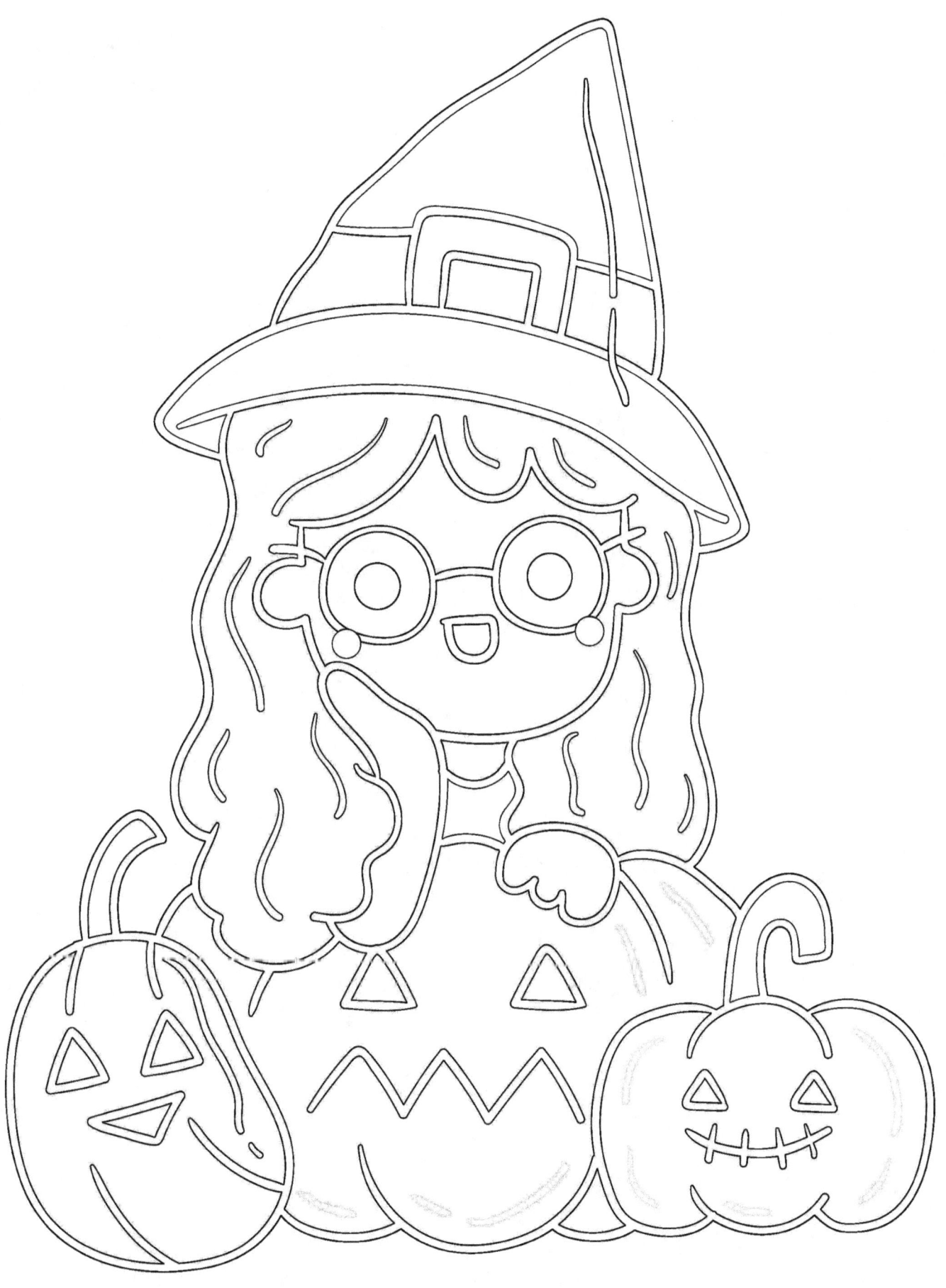

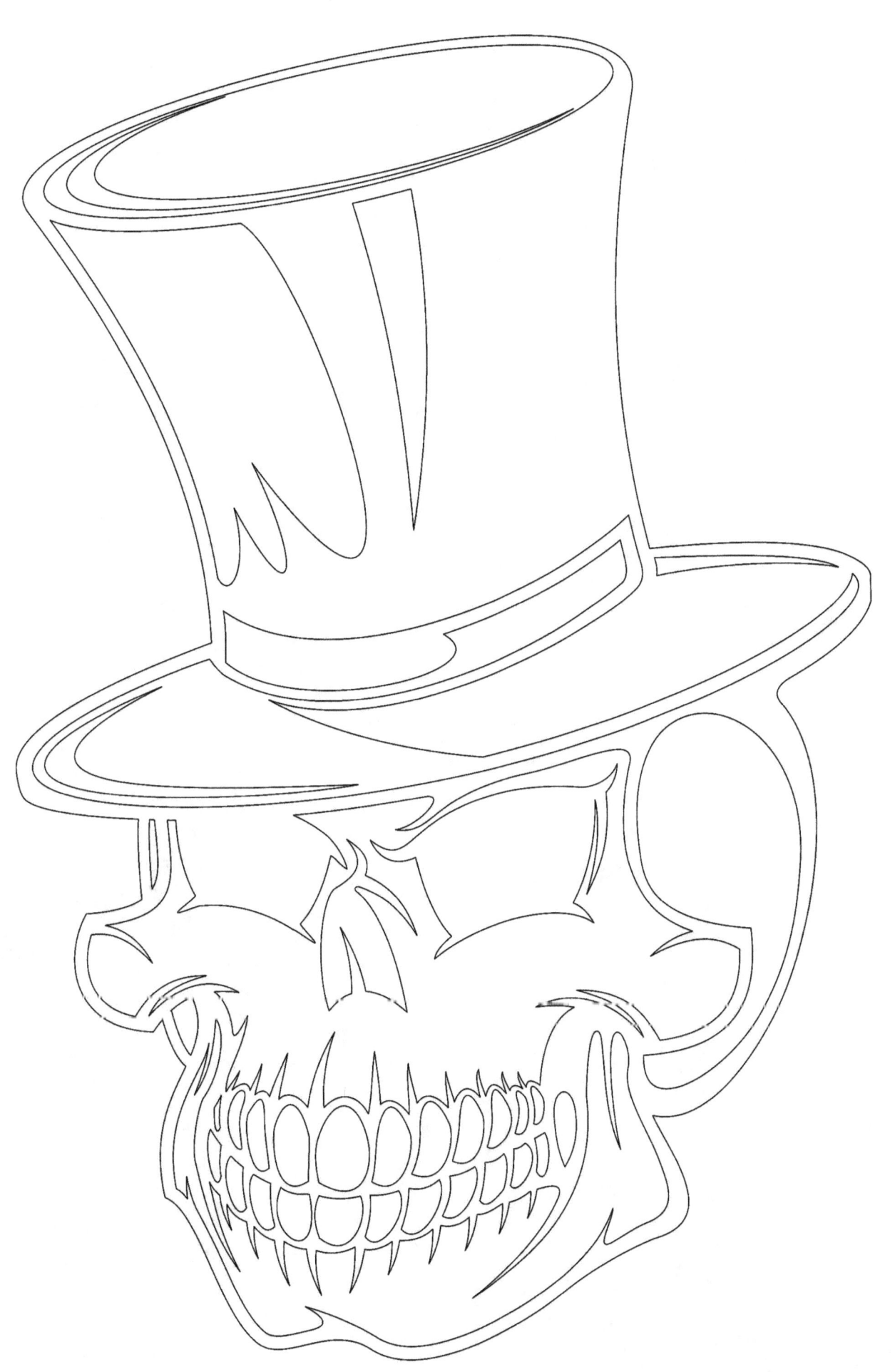

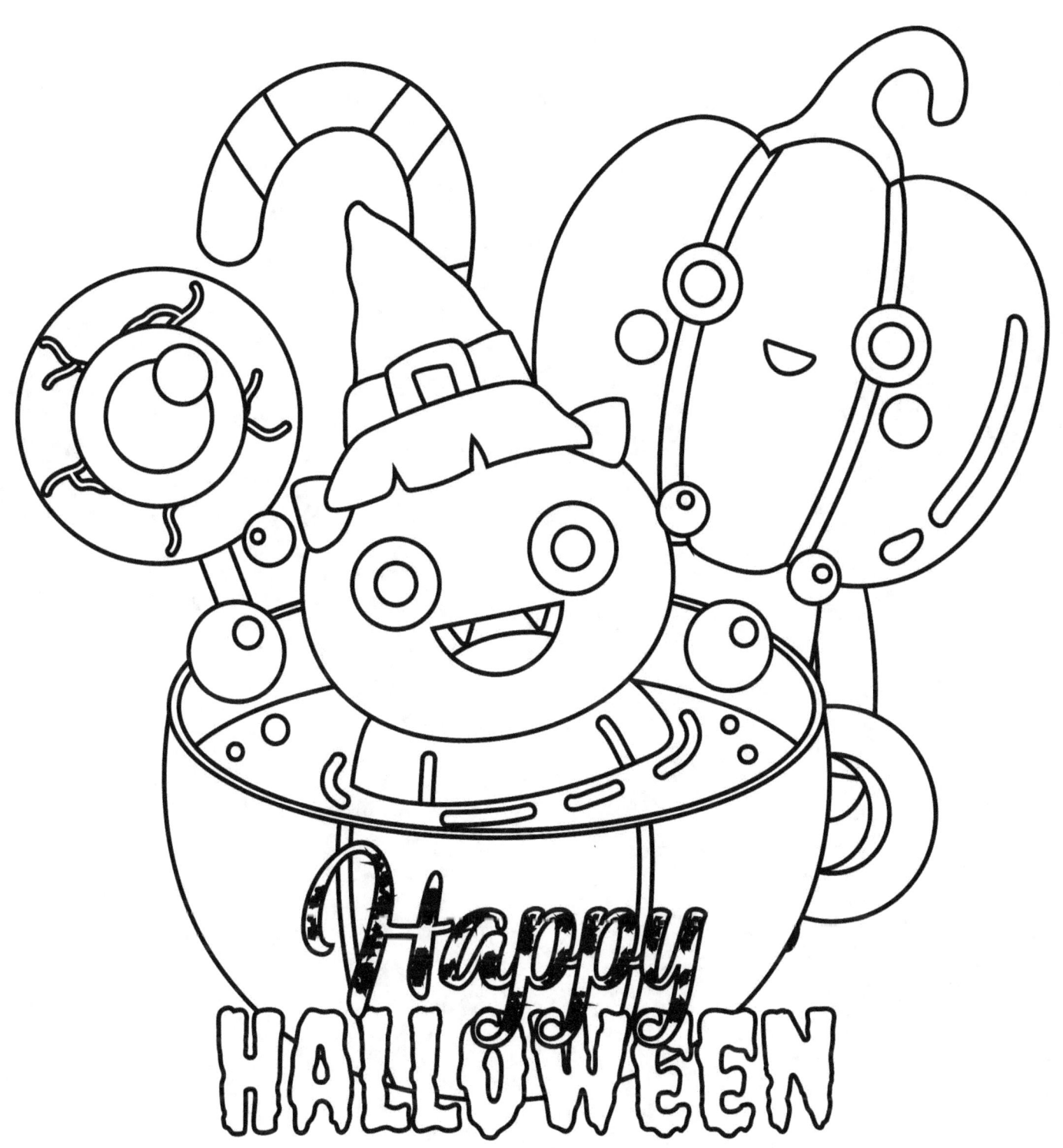

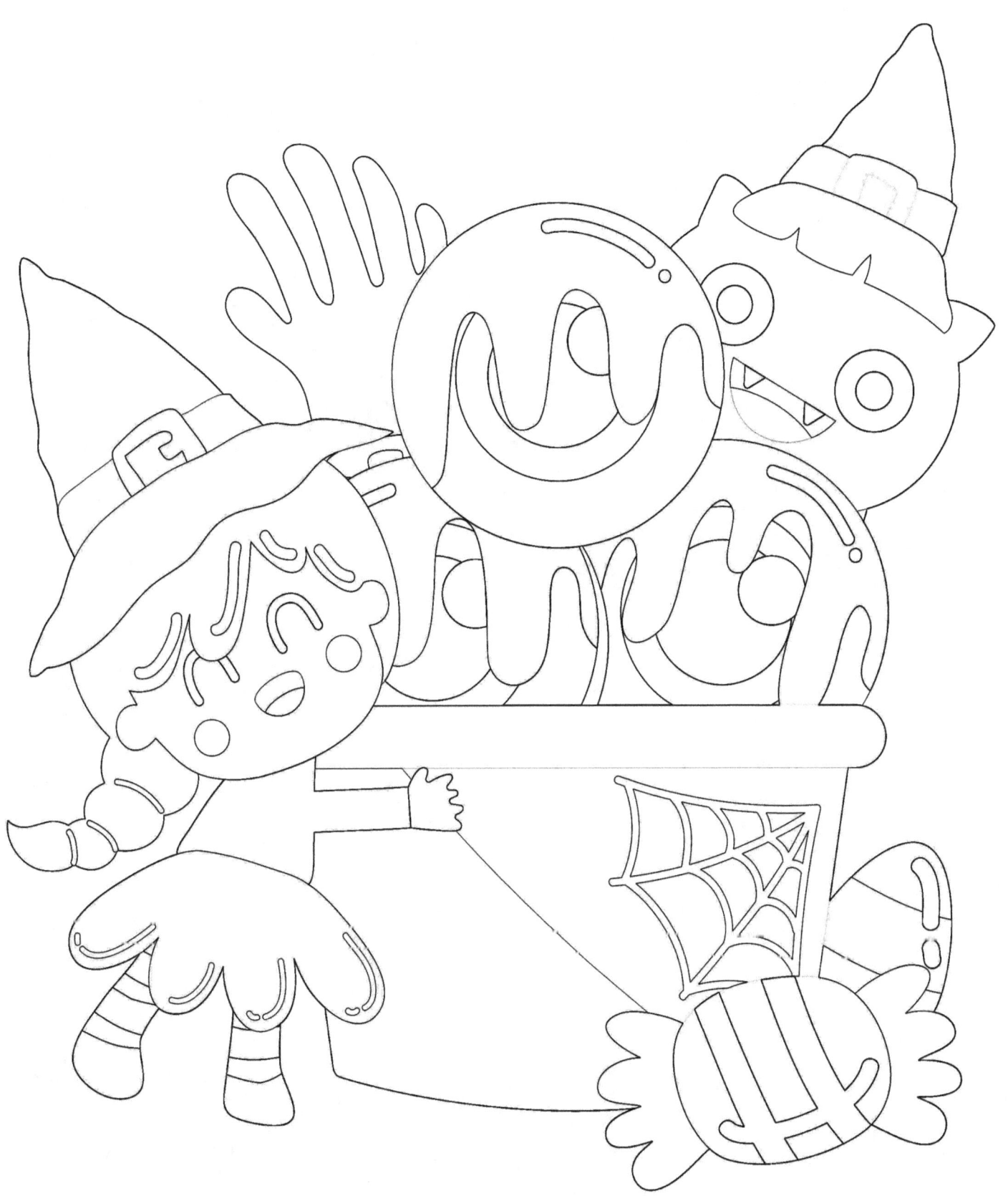

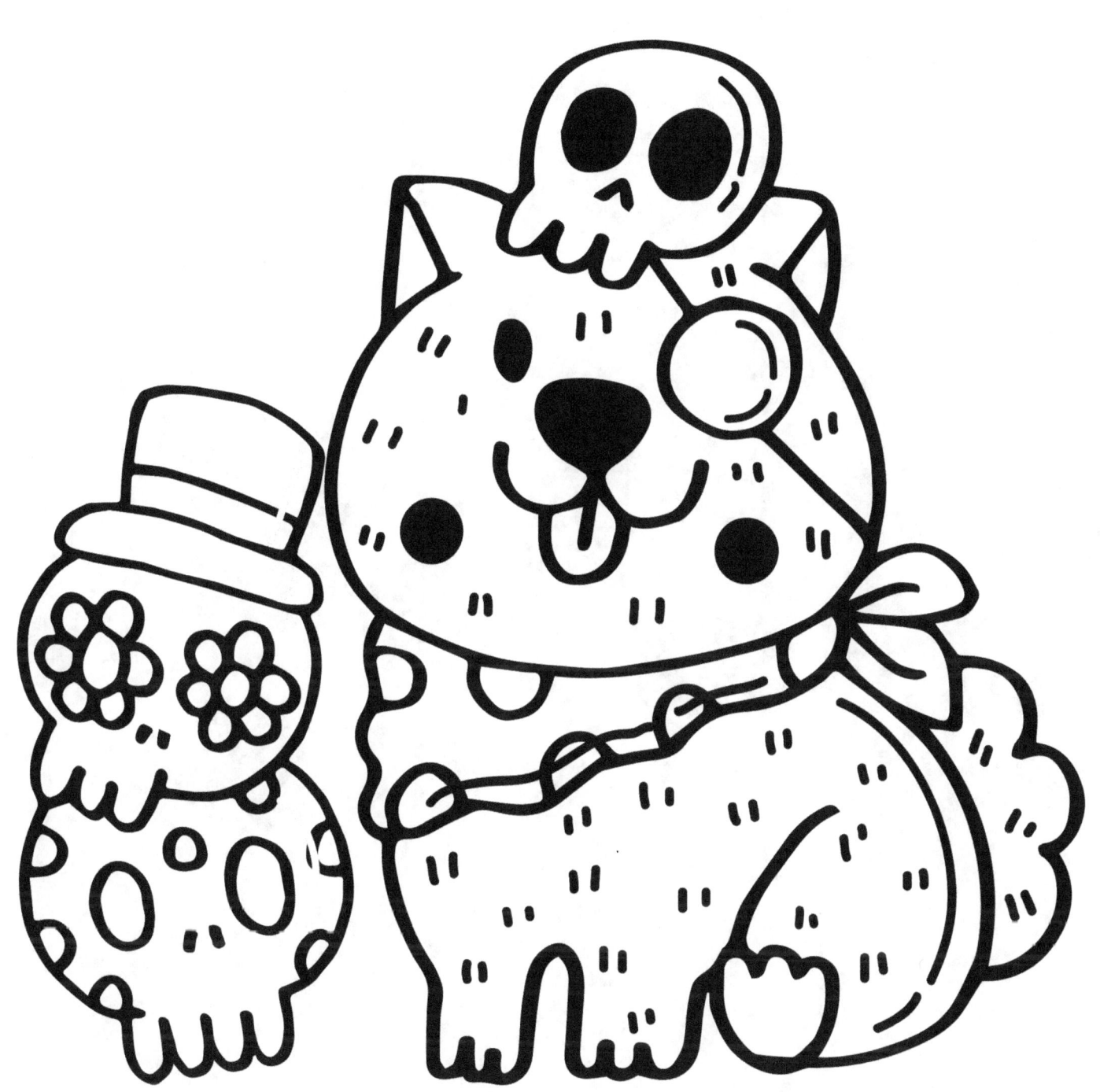

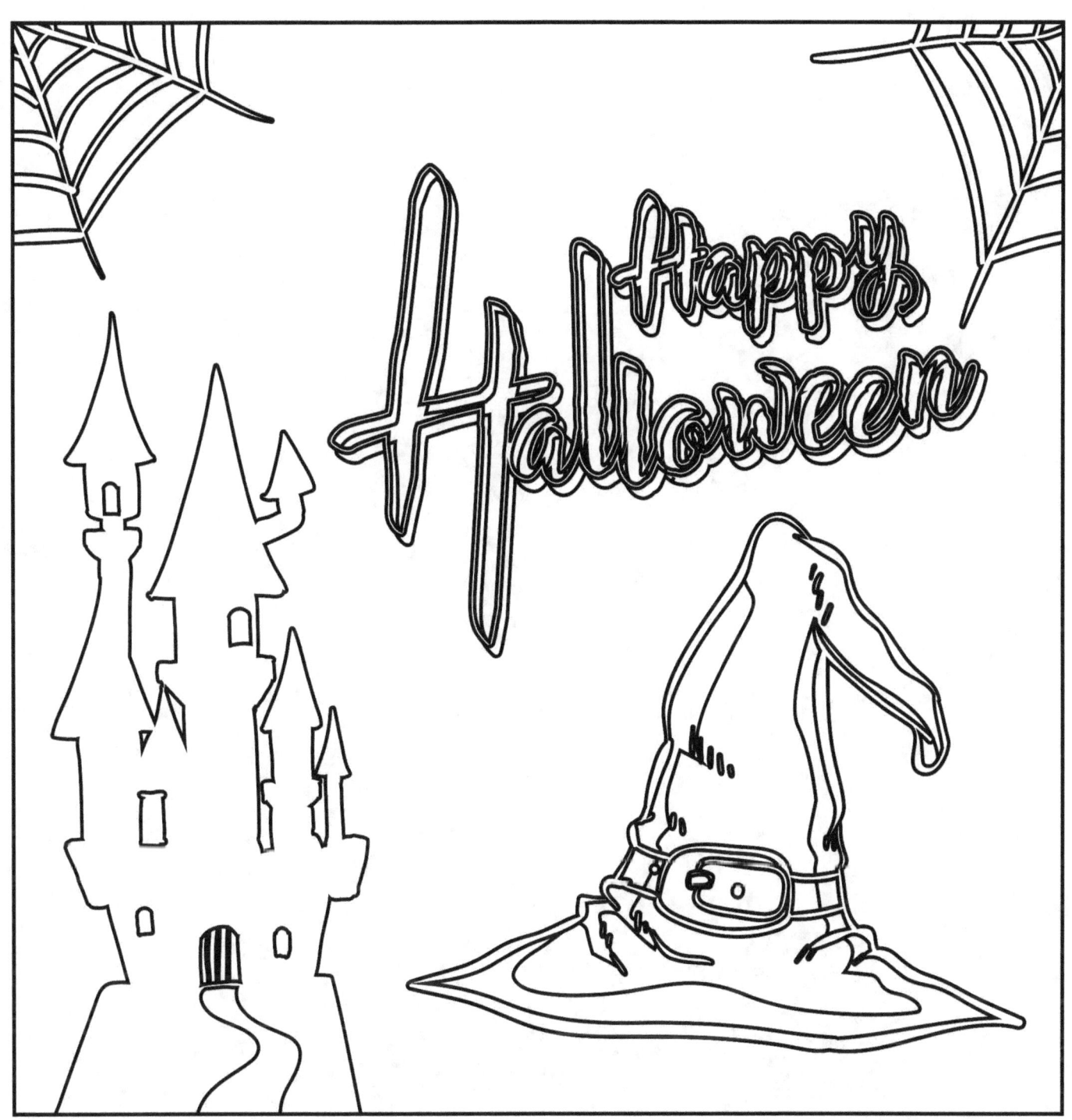

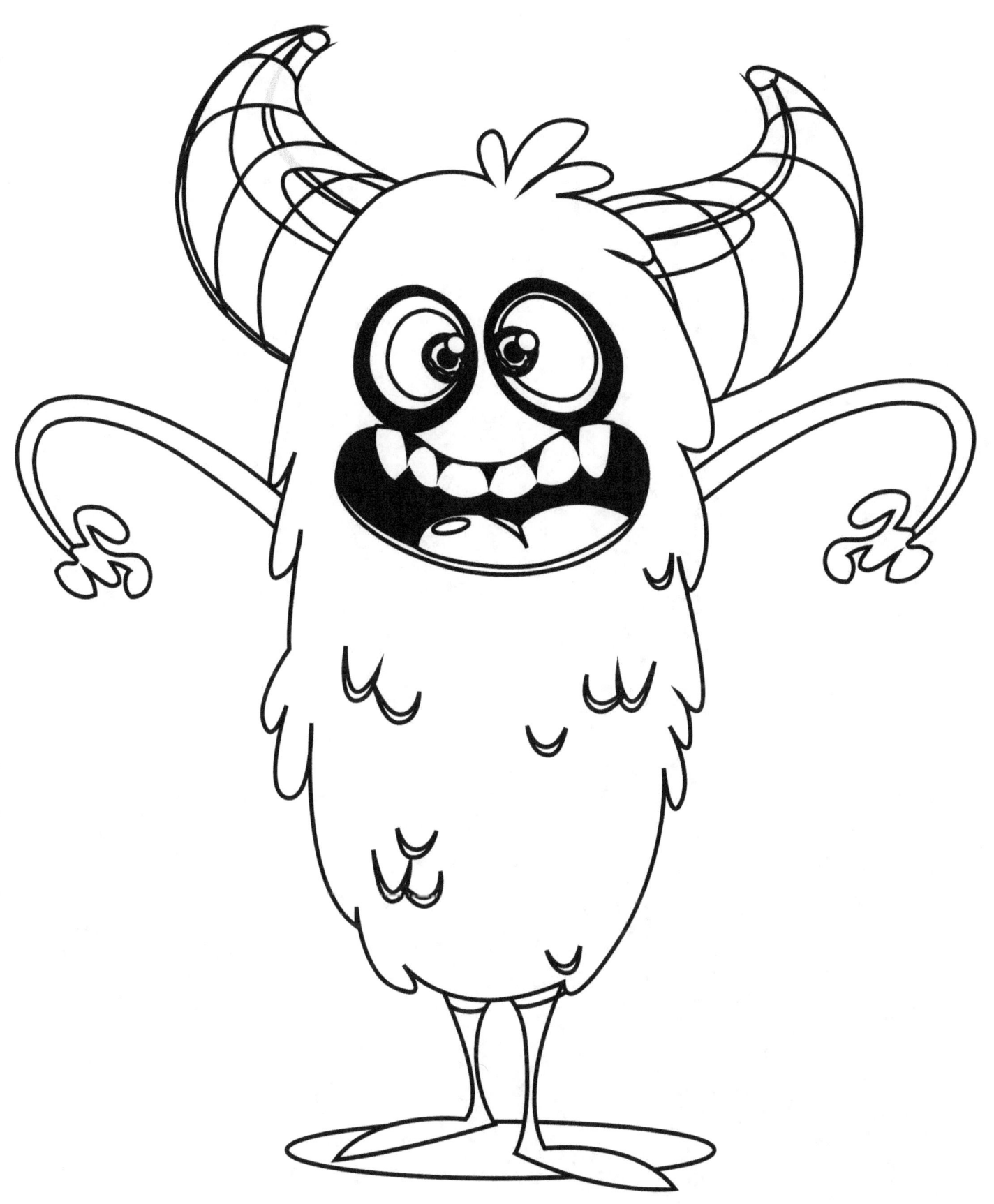

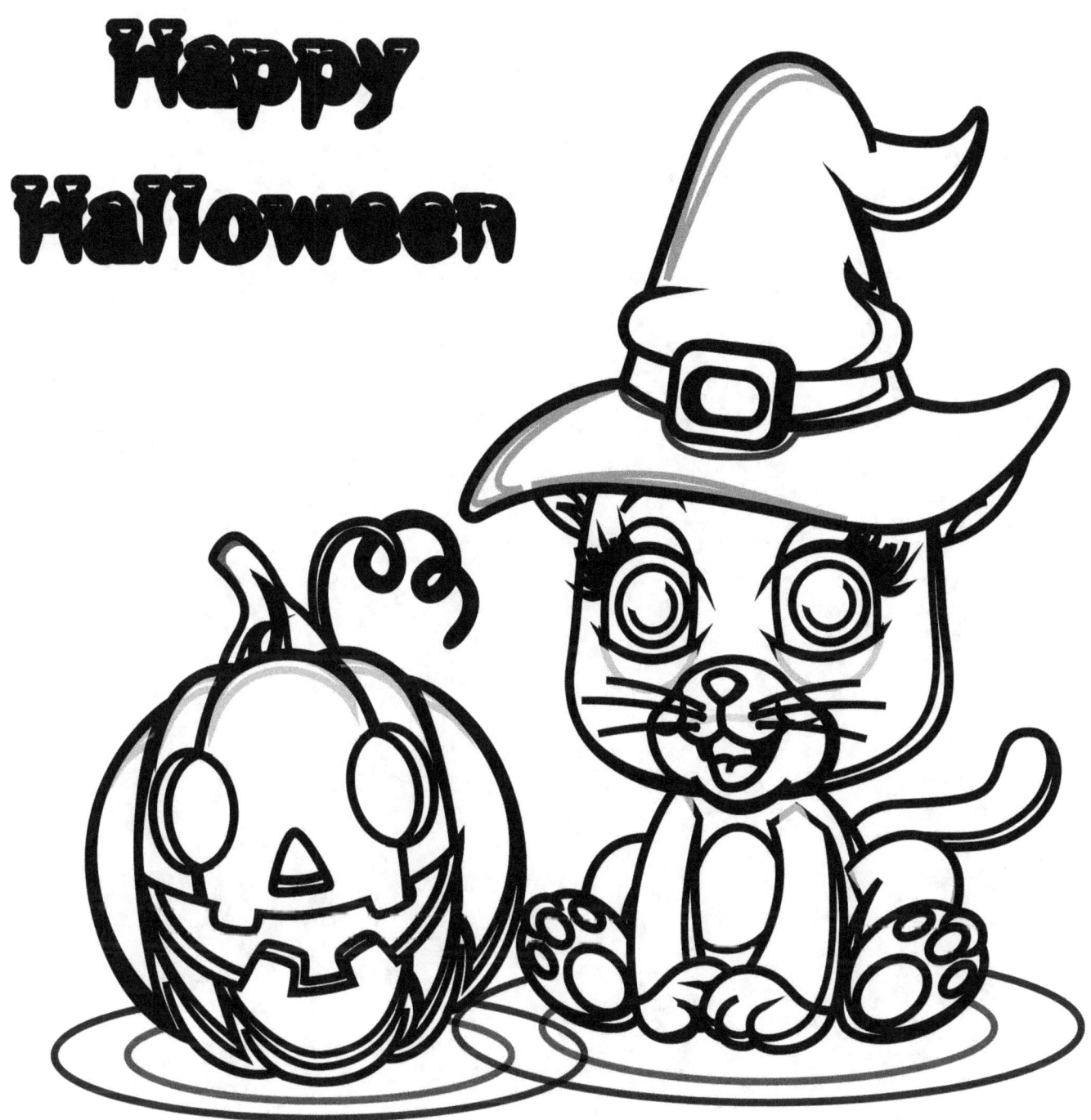

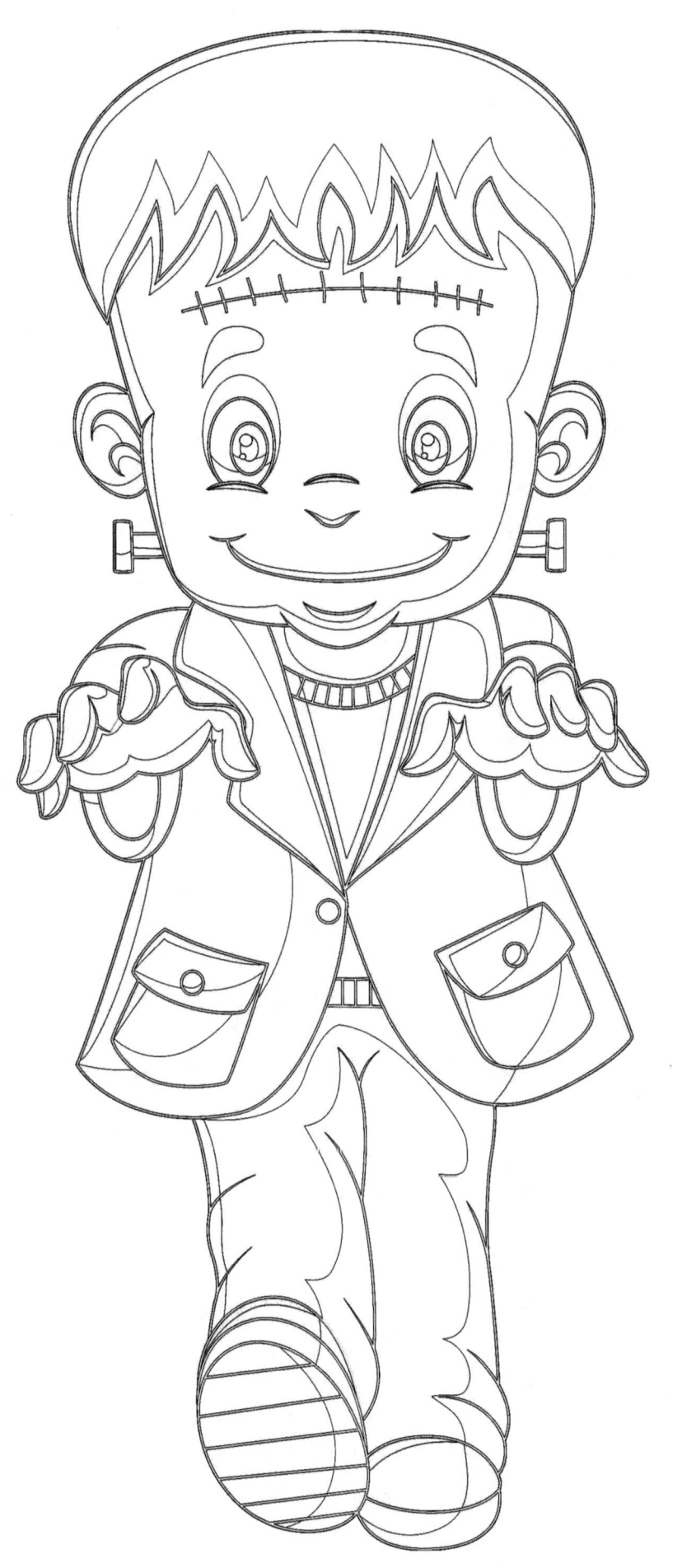

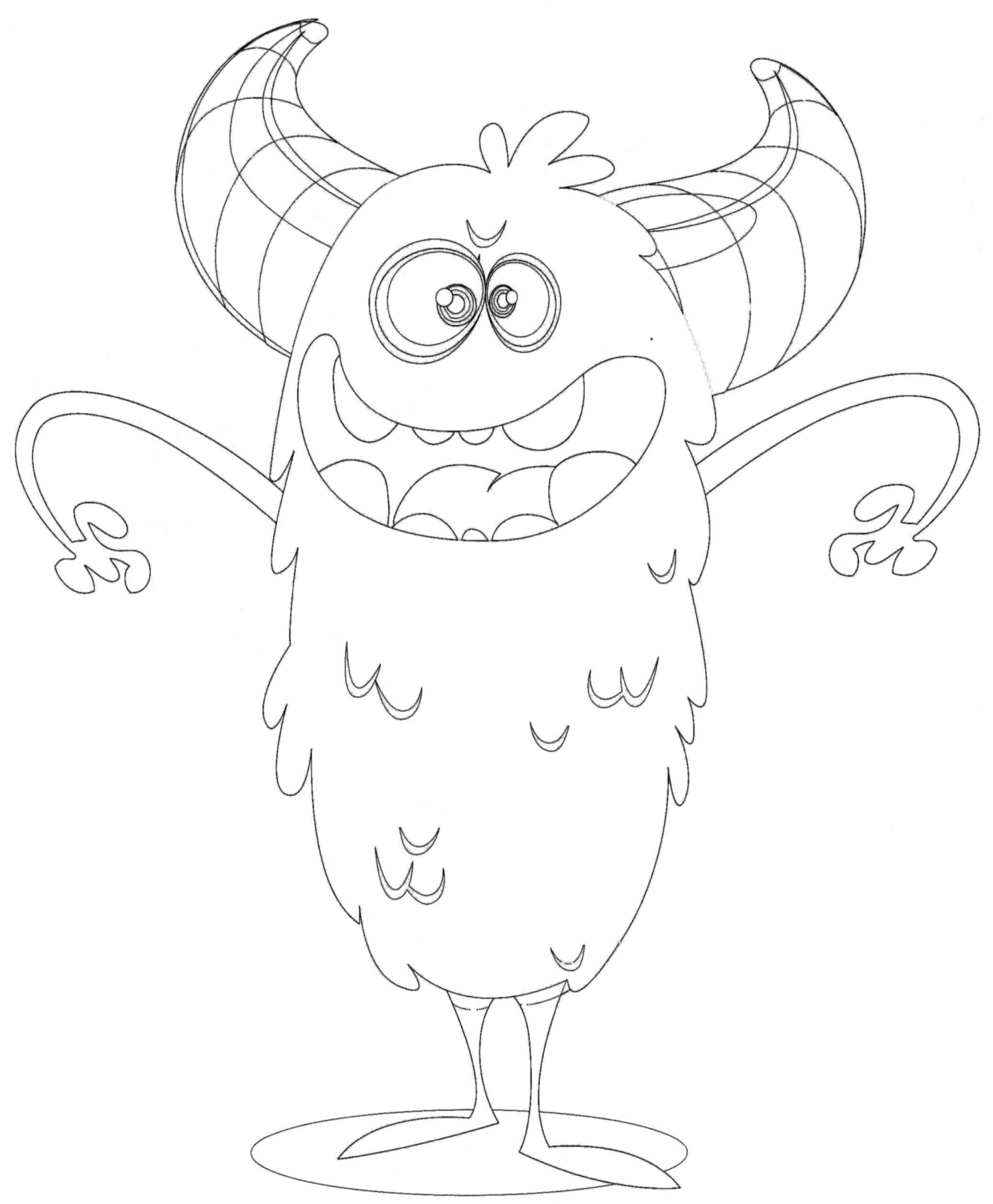

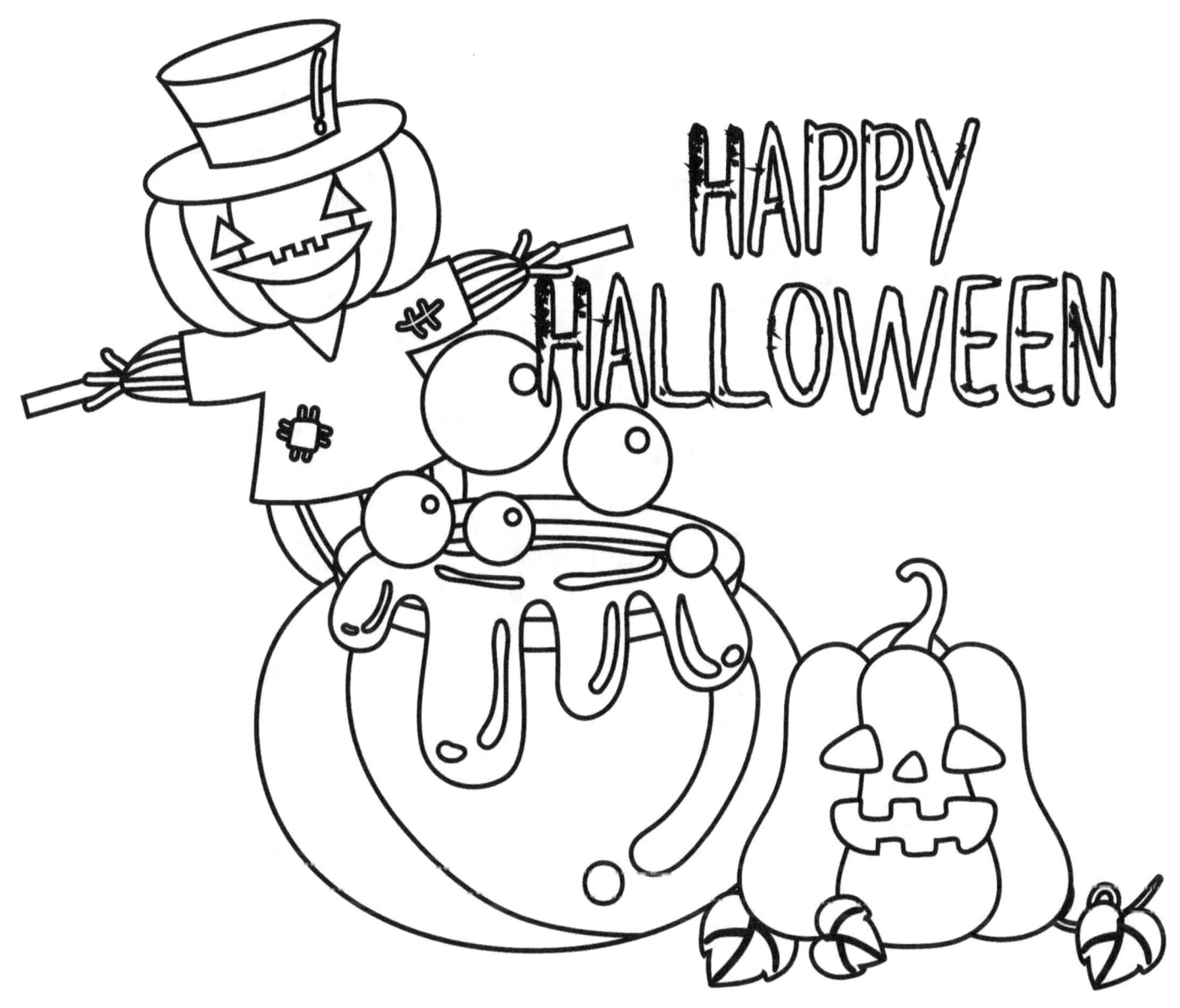

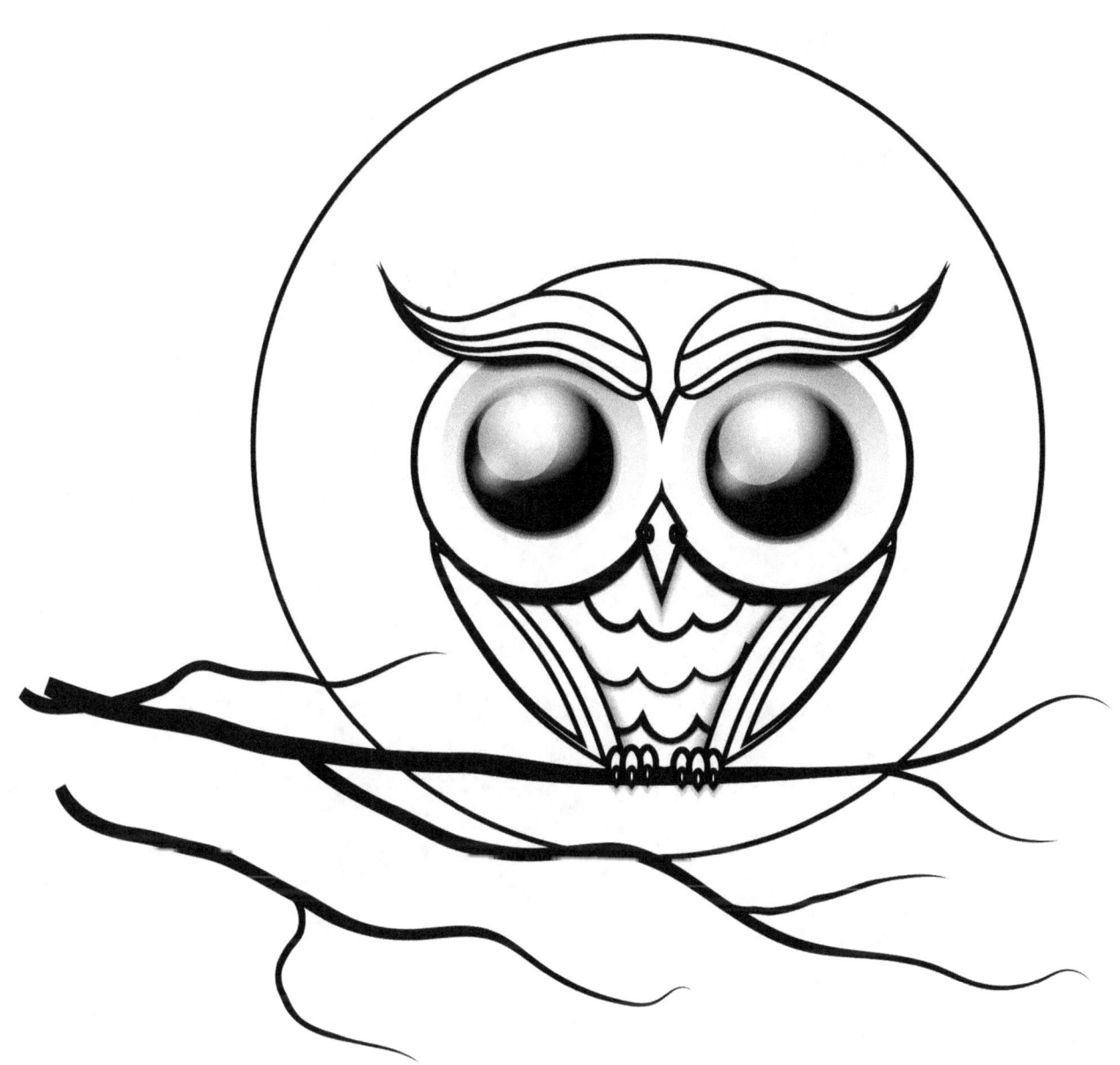

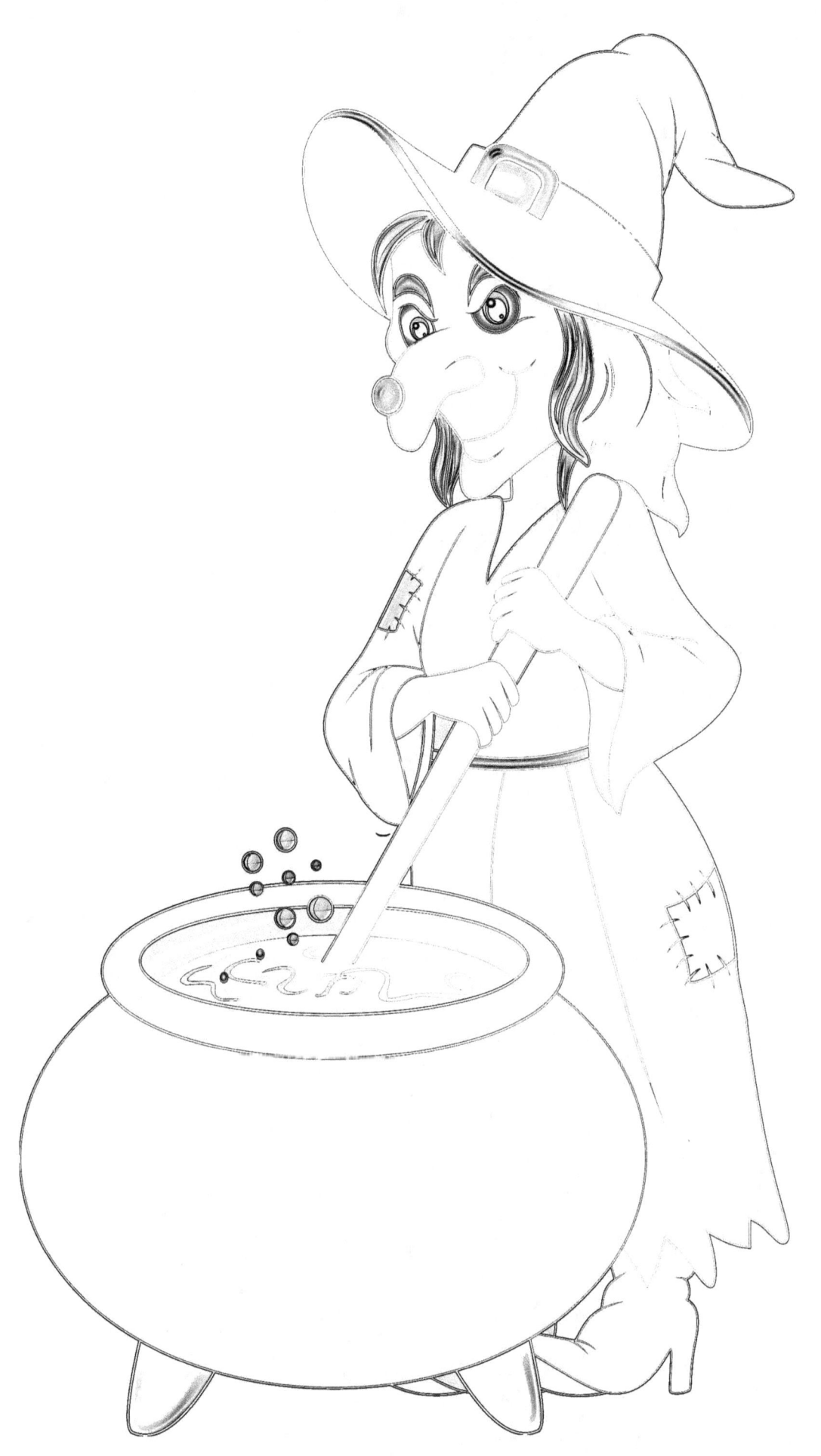

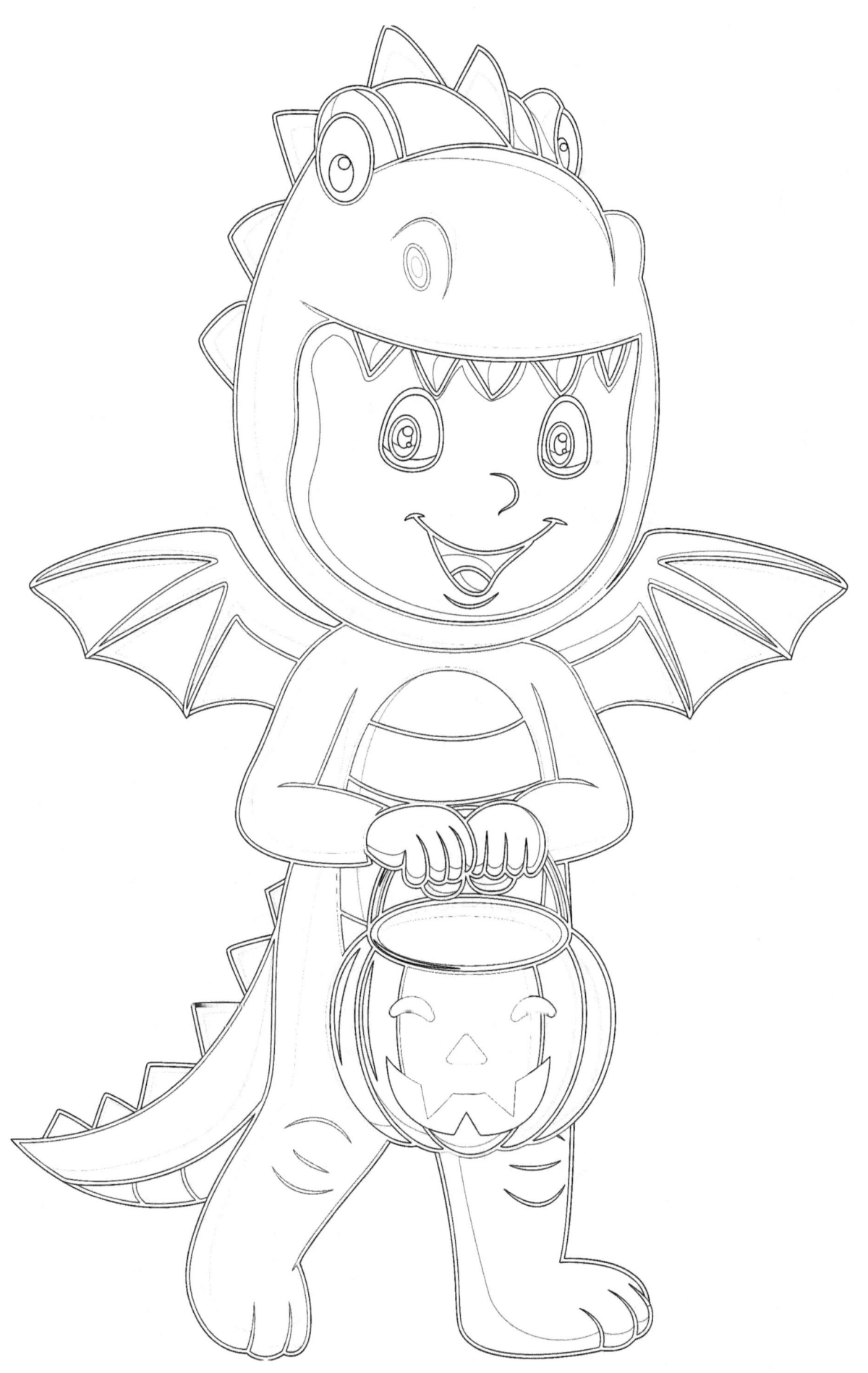

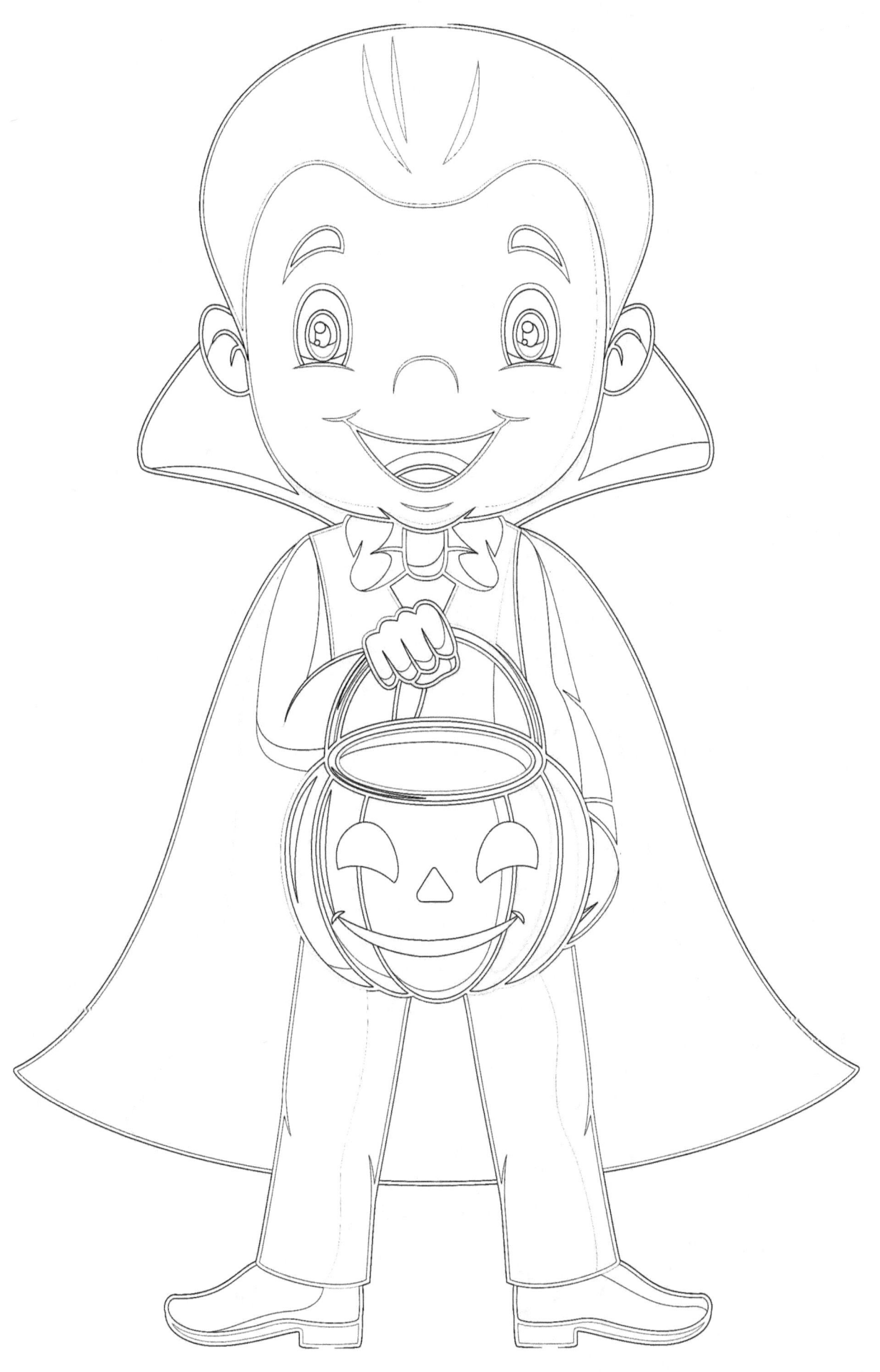

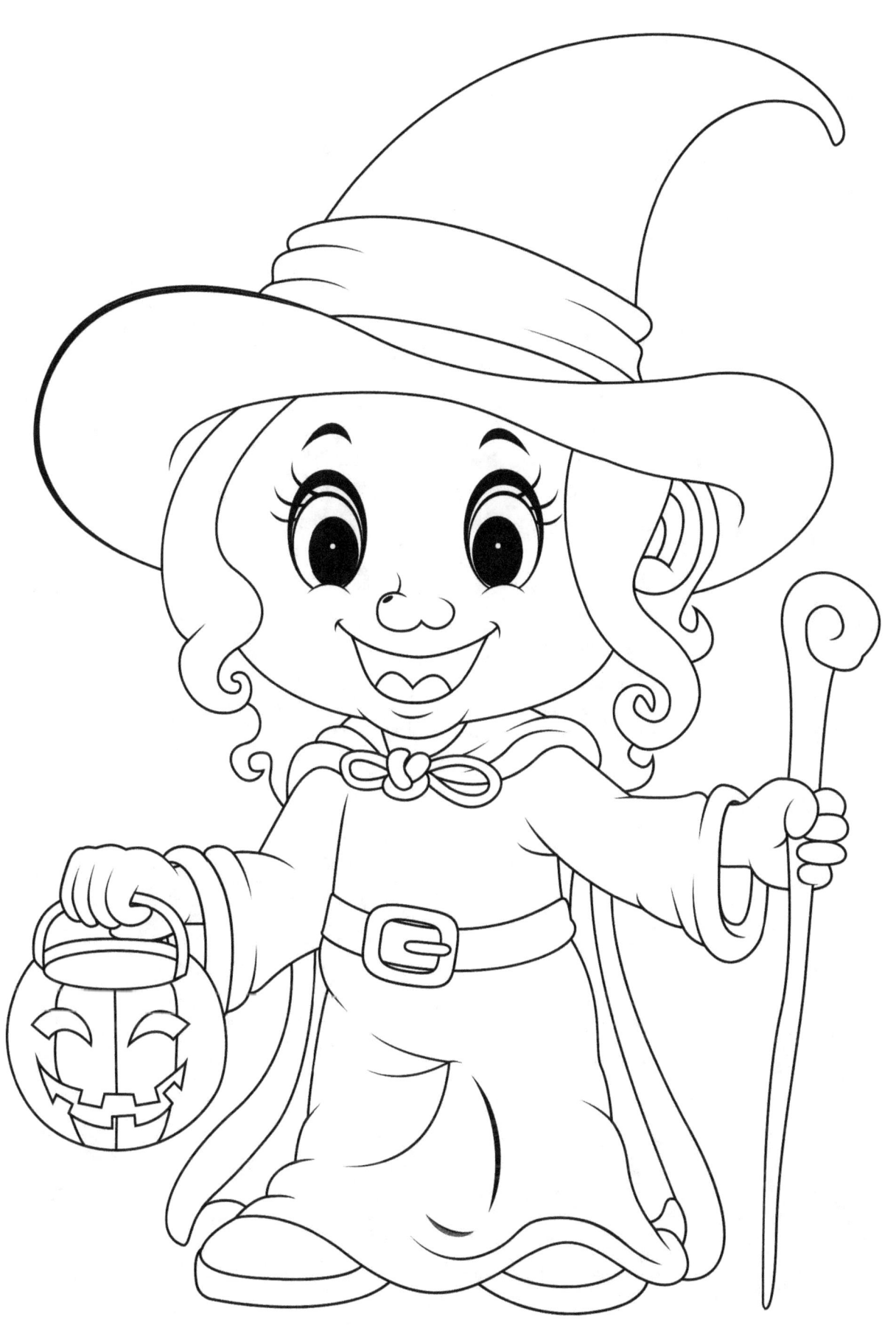

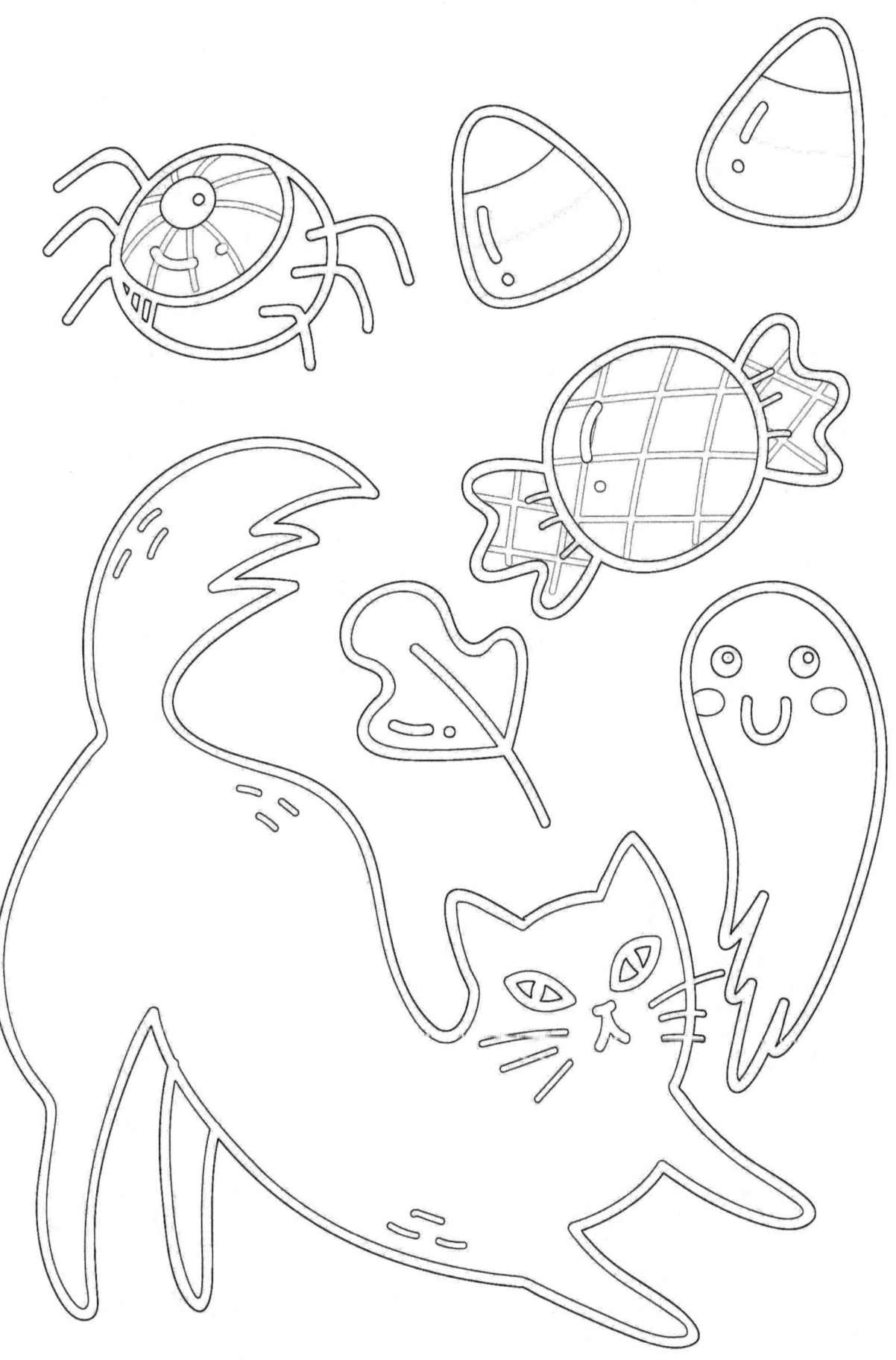

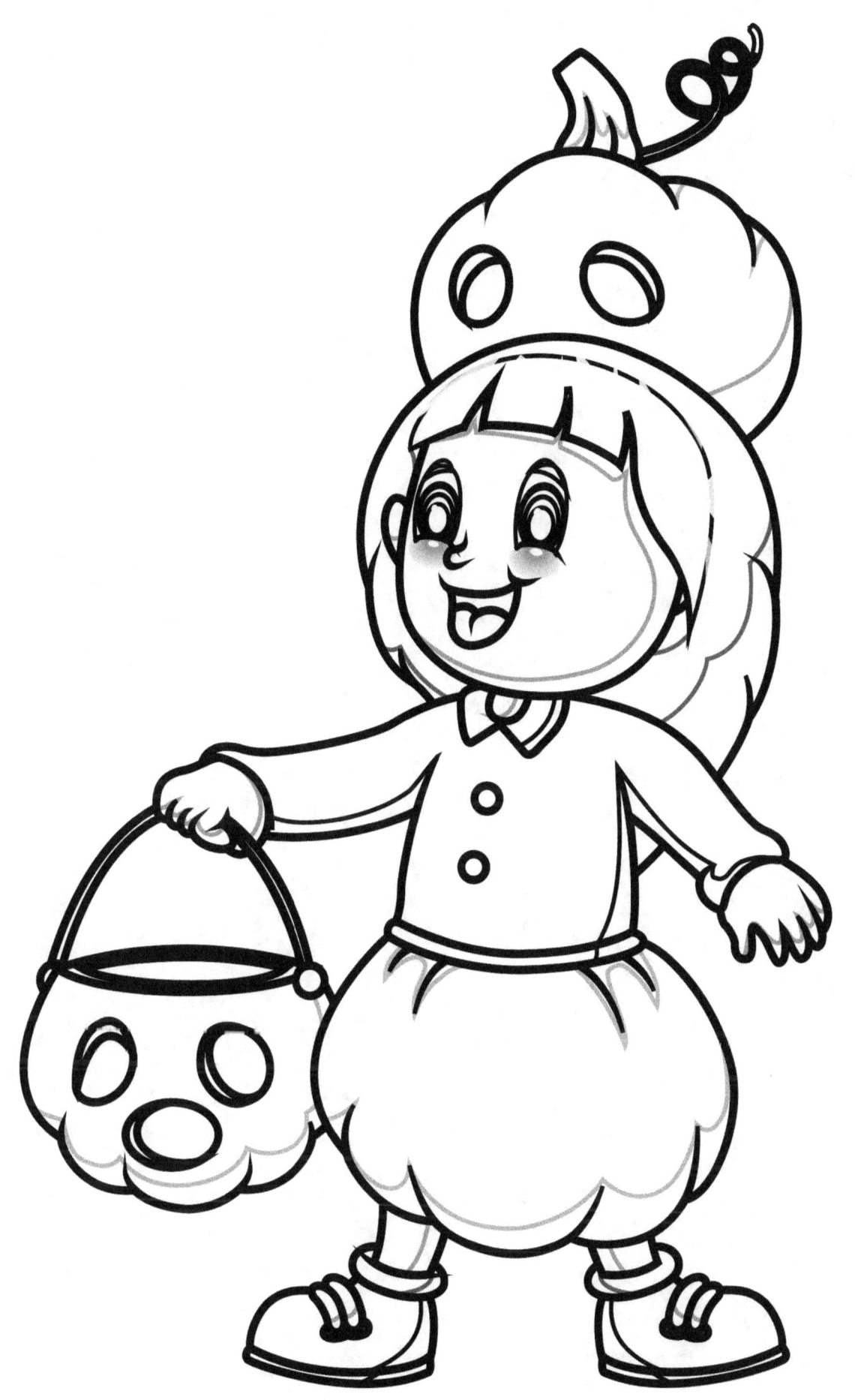

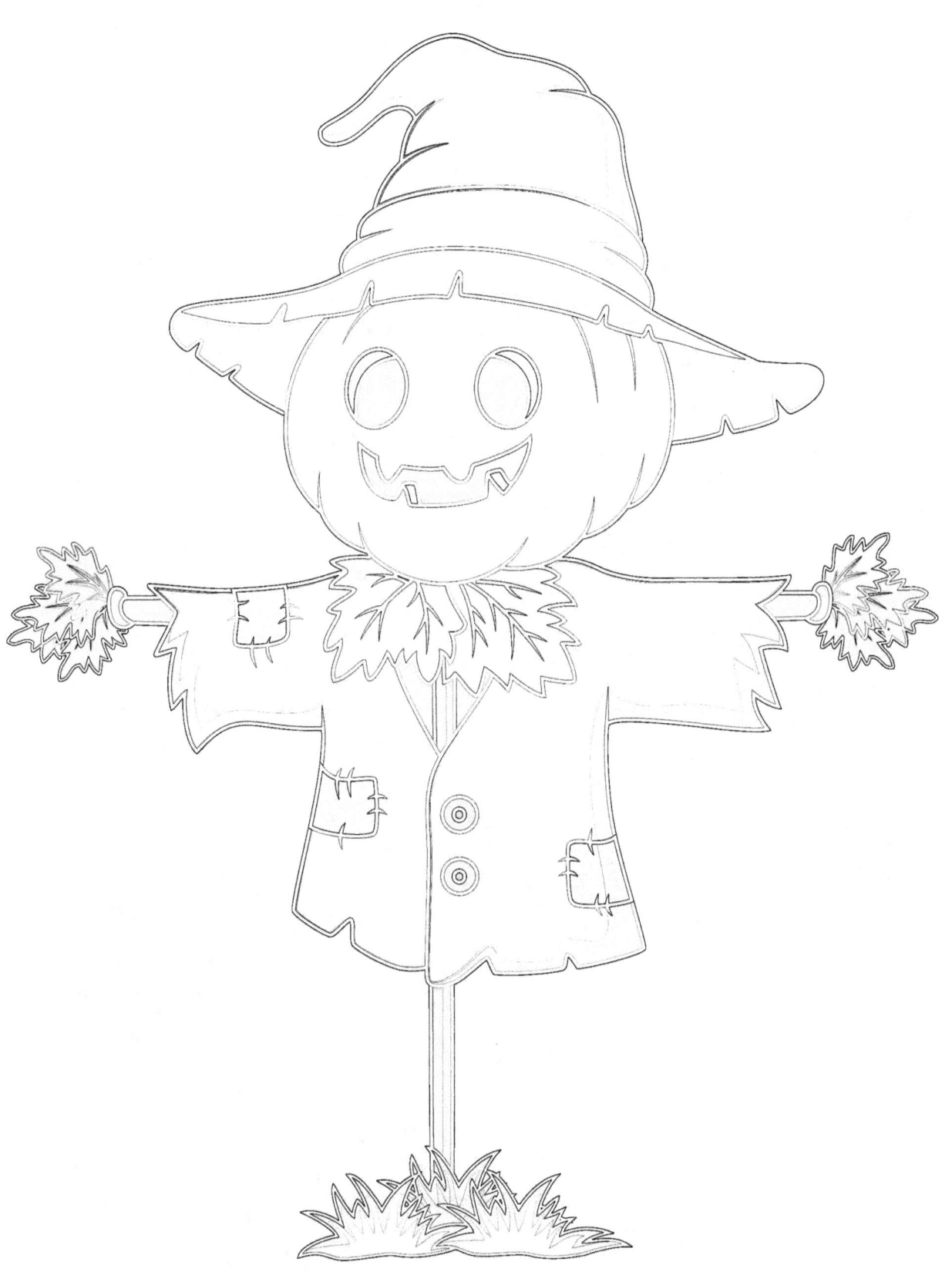

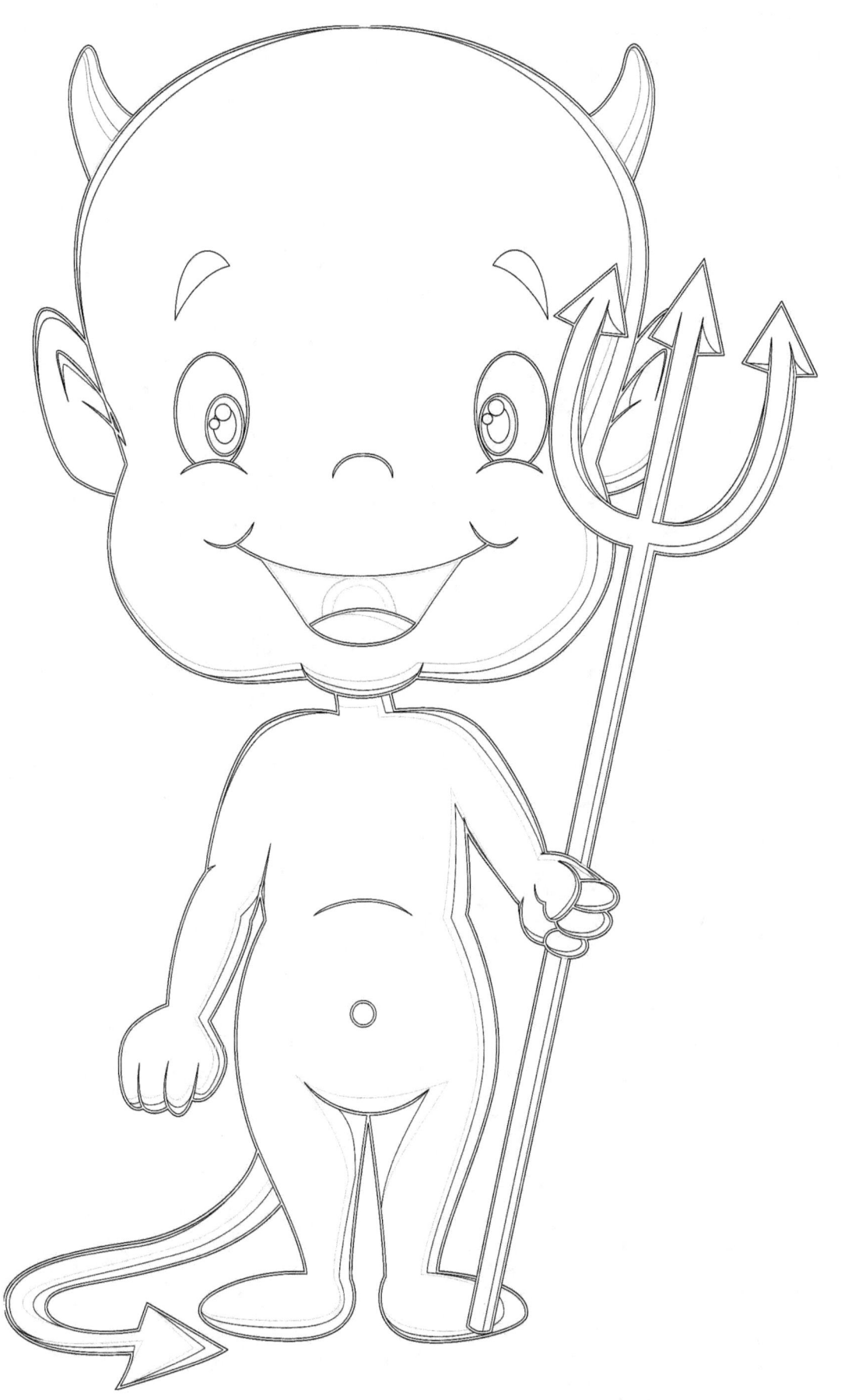

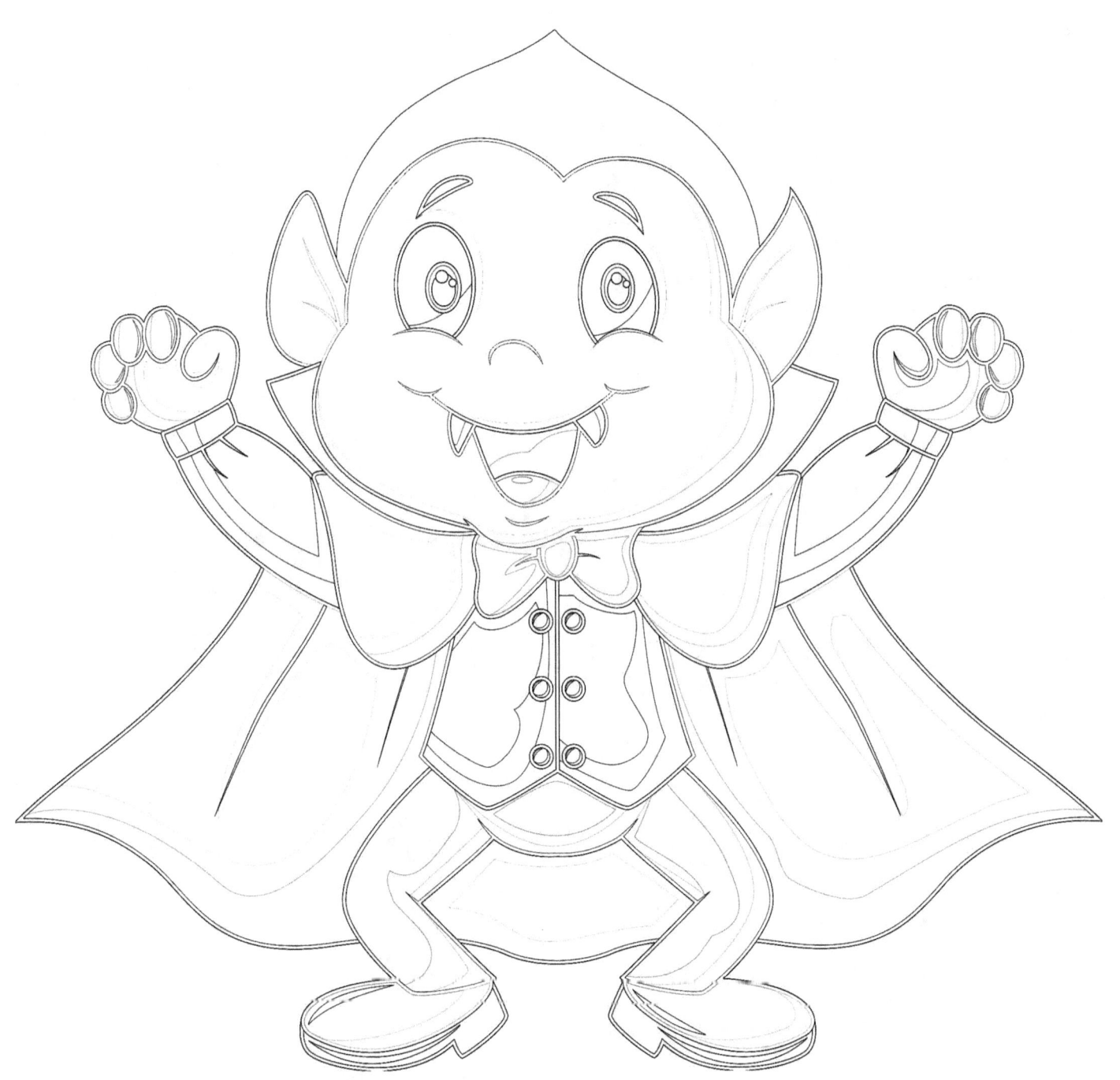

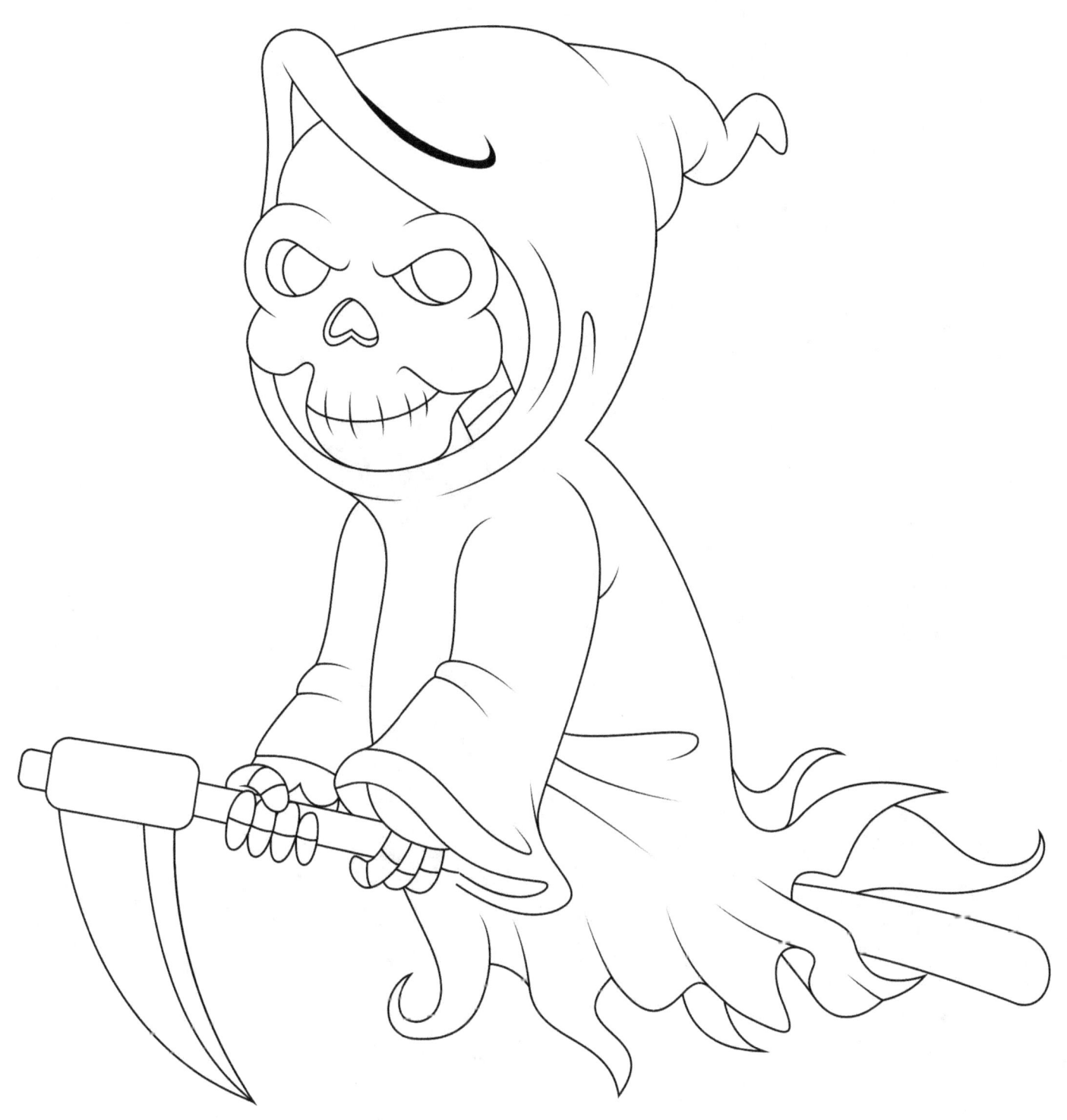

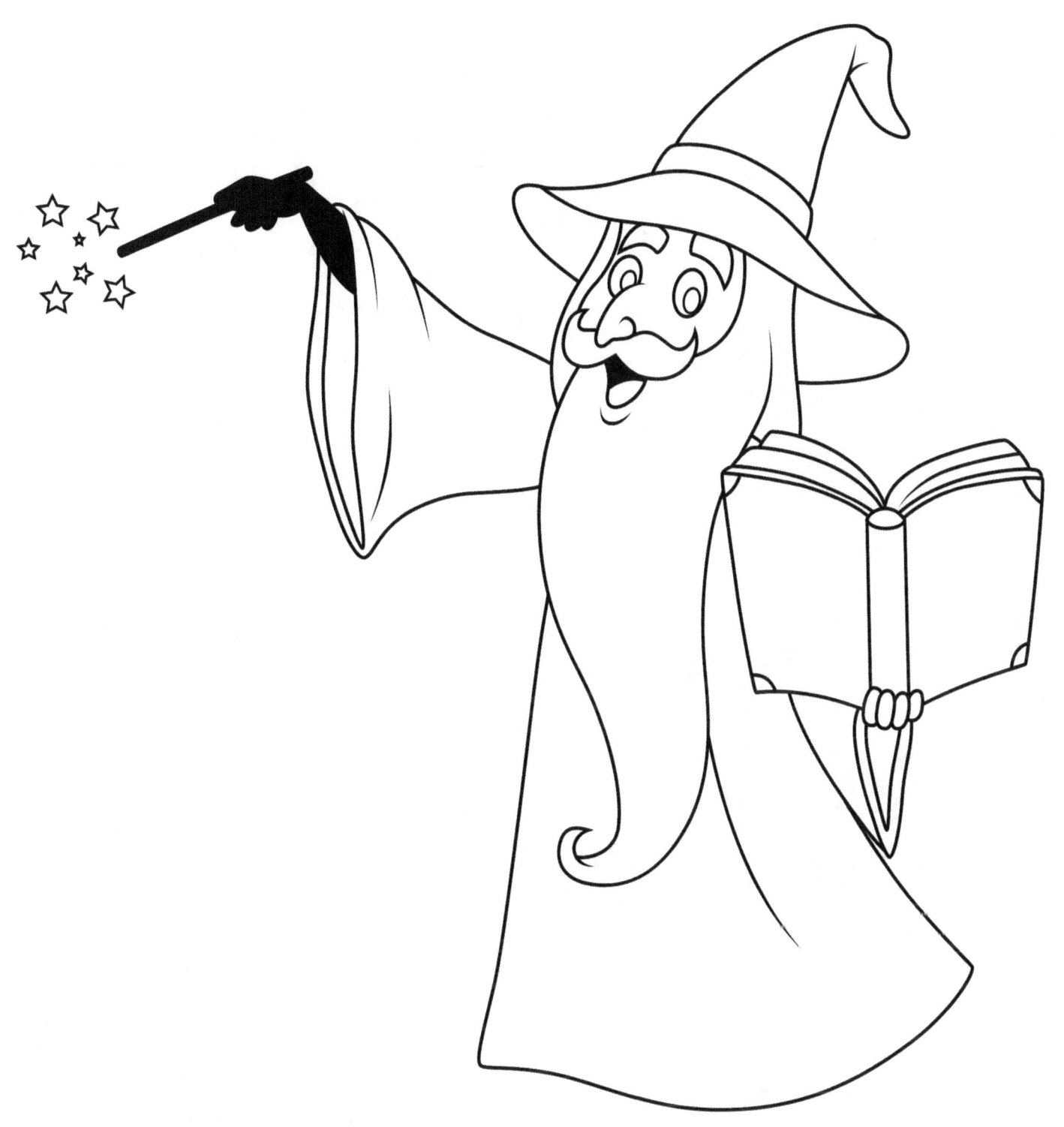

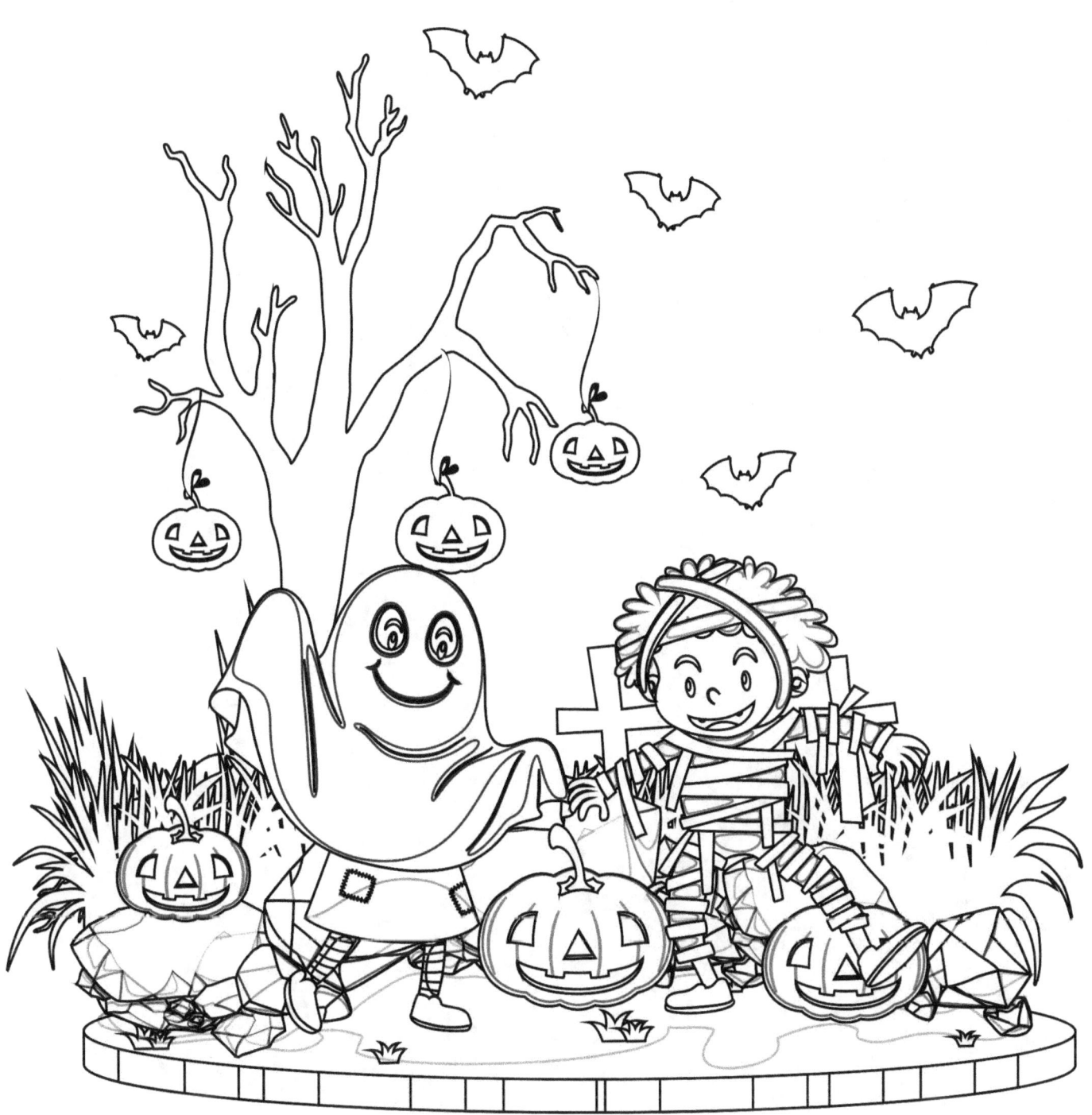

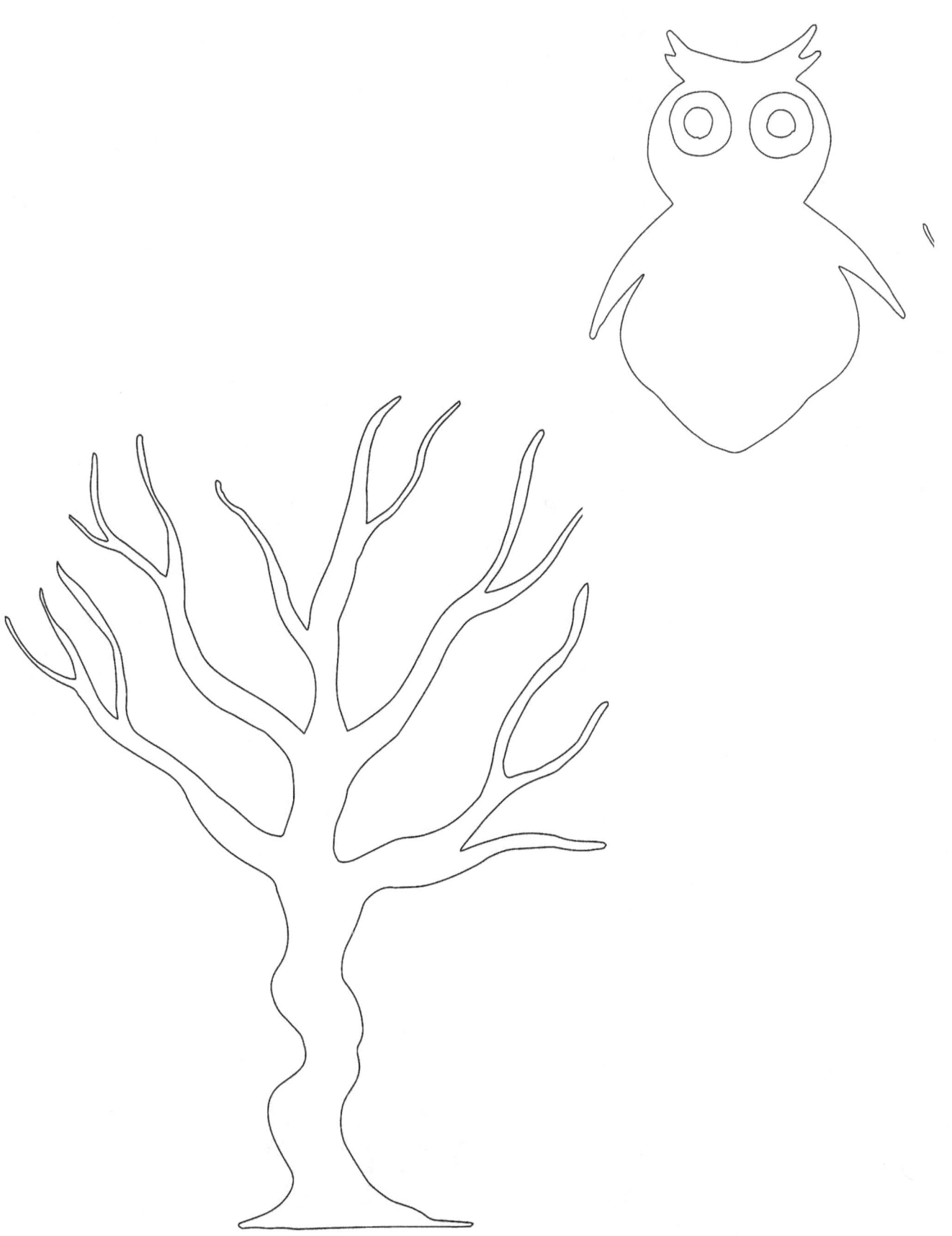

www.ingramcontent.com/pod-product-compliance
Lightning Source LLC
Chambersburg PA
CBHW080600220526
45466CB00010B/3208